The Competently Quirky Parables of an Eccentric Master Gardener

Rosie Kern

A Note from Rosie

Some people plant a few flowers. Some grow veggies in summer. Maybe they have a little spider plant or bamboo in the office.

I am not exactly one of those people. My philodendron extends from one pot on a shelf across three walls in my dining room. The Maple sapling in my front yard cries when temperatures top 100 degrees. Starbucks baristas across the city save coffee grounds for me. Plant catalogs choke my mailbox and, yes, this 69 year old Master Gardener owns a tractor.

I can get somewhat obsessive about it all. My husband has grown accustomed to my insistence that vacations must be planned around key times for vegetable garden harvesting. I write two page long watering instructions for house sitters in the fervent desire that leaving for a week won't destroy the charm and beauty of my home environment.

My unusual methods of approaching the challenges of the garden are effective, and I've given lectures for gardening clubs on various aspects of gardening from creating microclimates in high desert areas to vacuuming squash bugs. My friends smile and call me eccentric, fellow gardeners acknowledge me as competent and my kids just think I'm kinda quirky.

Comments from prereaders:
From Fil Chavez, author of "Unused Towels"
MAD MAD MAD . . . with lots of really good advice!
I am not a serious gardener, I am more of a "Well, I tried but ..." Nonetheless, this is indeed CRAZY MAD HUMOR ... i.e., "squash bugs .... Horniest critters in the insect world ... Live in a constant state of post-coital euphoria ... take a cold bath" and it gets better! It is definitely worth getting the book. Thanks, Rosie!

◊◊◊◊◊

Parris Afton Bonds , Internationally Published Romance Author
THE THRILL OF IT ALL ~ EVEN THE MANURE
Rosie Kern entertains with humor the agony and ecstasy of her gardening experience. Whether you are a gardening afficionado or not, you will enjoy her foray into her passion for gardening

◊◊◊◊◊

D. E. Williams   *Humorous take on gardening in the High Desert*
Rose Kern has a delightful way of writing that brings freshness to the technical aspects of gardening. Thanks for sharing your skill and your humor, Ms. Kern!

◊◊◊◊◊

Michael   *Hilarious yet educational take on gardening*
From the first sentence, Rosie has such an engaging style of writing, laced with humor. And if you're not careful, you might even learn something.

The Competently Quirky Parables of an Eccentric Master Gardener

Rosie Kern

The Competently Quirky Parables of an Eccentric Master Gardener©July 2024 Rose Marie Kern
All Rights Reserved.

For information about buying this title in bulk quantities or for special sales opportunities (which may include electronic versions), please contact rose@swcp.com

This book may not be reproduced, transmitted, or stored in whole or in part by any means, including graphic, electronic, or mechanical, without the express written consent of the author except in the case of brief quotations embodied in critical articles and reviews.

RMK Publications, LLC. PO Box 9761, Albuquerque, NM 87119
www.rmkpublications.com
Sponsored by Solar Ranch. www.solarranch.com

ISBN: 978-0-9985725-5-0
Library of Congress case number 1-14038941511

This book is dedicated

to my daughter, Melissa...

who owns the original Black Thumb

Contents

The Crazy Mad Gardener 1
When the S*** Hits the Fan! 5
Gardening: The Best Kind of Exercise 9
Chili or Chile ? 14
Chaos and Order 15
A New Way to Classify Weeds 19
Plants CAN Talk! 25
Queen of the Compost Holes 27
Petrichor 33
Water Challenges in Dry Climates 35
Plant Guilt Trips 39
The Heat is Coming! 45
Garden Water Systems 49
Dogs, Mates and Watering 53
And What About GRASS? 57
Gardening – Cheaper Than Therapy 59
Edible Gardens in Disguise 63
Gardening in Small Places 67
Things You Never Knew about Gardeners 71
The Black Thumb 75
Dirt, Sod and Daily Exercise 81
An Apology 83
Raised Garden Bed Repairs 86
Garden Microclimates 87
Cheapskate Garden Protection 93
Cold Frames and Row Covers 97

A Holiday Debacle 99
Cactus Christmas 104
Becoming a Master Gardener 107
Learning Pains 111
Innovative Garden Plant Containers 113
Creative Raised Beds 115
Raised Bed Gardening 119
I'm Looking Over… 123
Soil Sponges 125
Foresight and Solutions 127
Gads Zukes! 133
The Fabulous Flavors of Sunshine 137
Becoming a Solar Chef 142
Managing a Suburban Harvest 145
Vegetable and Herbs that dry easily: 150
Modify Your Garden Market Booth Tent 151
A Practical Environmentalist 155
Scavenger Gardening 161
Reuse Before Recycle. 173
Rosie Kern 179
Become a Master Gardener! 181

The Crazy Mad Gardener

This morning, I was wandering amongst the pumpkins and discovered – Squash bugs! Lots of them.

There is never just ONE squash bug; they always appear in a crowd. Half are climbing on the backs of the other half making MORE squash bugs. This grey shield-shaped Coreidae is the horniest critter in the insect world. Even their young are called nymphs!

Since squash bugs live in a constant state of post-coital euphoria, they don't move very fast, so you can just catch them by hand and dump them in a bucket of soapy water (Here, you oversexed cucurbit monster – take a cold bath!) But when it is already hot outside, that's a lot of extra work.

My methods are a lot quicker. I duck inside the house to grab a 100-foot extension cord and a Shopvac. (Did you know Shopvacs come in all sizes? I have three and the smallest only weighs about 6 pounds.)

Pulling back the leaves I target my quarry, then flip the switch, and WHOOSH, bugs gone. Of course, I do careful surgery on egg laden leaves afterwards.

***

It's Dad's fault.

As a kid my Dad had me help him plant some seeds. At the store, he picked out some tomato bedding plants for himself then let me choose a packet from the flower section. I chose Bachelor Buttons. I was right there  with him as he dug up a small area in our suburban backyard – pulled away the grass and chopped up the dirt. We opened the small packet of seeds and very carefully spread them on top, then covered those tiny things with a thin layer of dirt. Then we watered and waited. Those were probably the best watered seeds in the state of Indiana. When the first little spears poked up, I was disappointed – it just looked like regular old boring grass. Dad told me that a lot of plants start out looking like that – he said "Be patient." The little green shoots pushing upwards grew incrementally every day larger and larger, and OH MY!

One day I went out to look and the first flower had opened up. That day, I became a lifelong gardener.

In truth, I can get somewhat obsessive about it all. My husband has grown accustomed to my insistence that vacations must be planned around key times for vegetable garden harvesting. I write two-page-long instructions on watering for house sitters in the fervent desire that leaving for a week or two won't destroy the charm and beauty of my environment.

I was transferred several times over my 34-year career – which meant that I have bought and sold several properties, mostly near the airports in larger metropolitan areas. When contacting a realtor, my first order of business was to emphasize that I NEEDED a big yard.

Yes, NEEDED, not just wanted. They say that Air Traffic Control is a stressful job – it was one I was good at and enjoyed, but when I went home, I had a great outlet for any angst. All it takes is a chipper-shredder and a compost heap

Out come the clippers! Time to go after those dead branches prune the roses and the trees. Rip those *$%@! WEEDS out of the ground. Then fire up the chipper-shredder. Grab the branch, thrust it into the hopper, and all the frustrations are loudly stuffed, chopped, and mulched into little itty-bitty pieces. Once that pile is reduced to slivers, you take the bag off and dump it into the compost pile.

No more stress.

Yes, my favorite piece of garden equipment is a chipper-shredder. When I am angry, upset, or just frustrated, my therapy involves ripping weeds out of the ground or trimming bushes and branches. Then the chipper is rolled out and I visualize whatever the heck is bothering me as I thrust the mounds of innocent vegetation into the hopper. The angry roar of the motor and whirling blades complement my emotional turmoil, and the tiny fragments of torn organic matter spewing from the side release my built-up frustration.

In the fall, I hook up a small utility trailer to my Subaru. Stealthily, I cruise the quiet streets of middle-class suburbia until – there! I see a pile of what appears to be bags of leaves set on the sidewalk, waiting for Tuesday's trash pickup. I pull up to the curb and do a perfunctory walk up to the front door. I do ring the bell and ask permission to take the bags, but if no one is home...well, heck, nobody sets trash bags on the street unless they want to get rid of them...right?

Eight bags here, twelve bags there...by the time I am done, the little trailer is crammed five feet high with leaves, and I am on my way home to my chipper and my compost heap. I am the Queen of leaf thieves, and as added value, I stop off at one or two, or maybe all, the Starbucks in the northeast quadrant of town, and snarf all the little silver bags full of used coffee grounds left out for area gardeners.

I spend hours watering with a hose in my hand rather than hooking up a sprinkler just so I can walk through the garden and listen to the plants sigh with pleasure as the droplets caress their leaves. There is a wonderfully pungent, almost burnt aroma unique to dry, hot soil released by the touch of water.

In this book look for some amusing stories and unique insights into gardening. Planting, harvesting, and just being a part of the garden are all here – ENJOY!

At the end of a good gardening day, my hands are dirty, my nails are broken, and I am completely relaxed and content with the world. Crazy is good.

***

When the S*** Hits the Fan!

Many of you fine Master Gardeners in New Mexico know that my company transferred me to the Washington D.C. area for about ten years. Before leaving, I had gotten the small front yard at my house in the sandy south valley built up so that my husband, Wolf, could walk barefoot on a grassy lawn. The raised beds had healthy, colorful flowers, shrubs, and vegetables.

Because I always intended to return to Albuquerque, my daughter, Melissa, housesat while we were exiled to the East Coast. I knew there would be casualties...Melissa has a black thumb...but I figured if 50% of my garden and yard survived, I would be lucky. So, with an admonishment to her to water regularly, I moved from my beloved desert to the former swampland that is our nation's capital.

I won't go into the extensive list of reasons I hated living there, though I will mention that the humidity is so intense you can cut the air with a knife. After three more moves, a decade later, I finally arrived back in Albuquerque. My front yard could have been a great showcase for the hardiness of drought-resistant plants. The lilac bush was not dead, barely. The two young pecan trees, however, were bare sticks that pulled easily from the ground. The Afghan pine was actually pretty healthy.

The lawn was...not. A few scraggly blades of grass pushed up in bare sandy patches or struggled to stay hidden in the shade of the hardier weeds that had invaded in my absence.

So, now I had two challenges. 1. How to bring back the small grassy area I planted for the corgi to roll in, and 2. How to get rid of the pigweed, goat's head, and London rocket. I'm still working on the weeds. I hit them with a flamethrower and some pure vinegar – I think they liked the vinegar. I didn't want to use other chemicals unless I had no other choice.

Bringing back the grass could crowd out the weeds, but that will take some doing. Since I came back in time for fall, I hitched up my faithful utility trailer and roamed the streets in the university area to find bags of leaves destined for the landfill. My trailer was filled in an hour, and I took it back to the south valley. From the time I got home, I'd been raiding Starbucks for used coffee grounds, and I bopped over to Home Depot to purchase ten bags of steer manure.

The challenge was to mix this all together and spread it evenly over the front lawn area. At this point, I had a brilliant idea – let my chipper-shredder do the work!

With all my bags of organic materials piled at one side of the yard I drug out my old friend. This enthusiastic rattletrap had been masticating yard trash for me since 1991. After doing a bit of maintenance, I pulled the cord and she fired right up.

Chipper-shredders have places to insert branches and leaves; after they are reduced to small pieces by a large whirling blade, they are spewed out. Most of the time, you put a tough bag on the end, capture the detritus, and take it over to wherever you want to pile it.

This time, I left the bag off the end of the chute, figuring it would scatter it all across the yard.

It worked great! I set the unit up to shoot in a certain direction, then dumped in a bag of leaves, a bag of coffee grounds, and a bag of manure. Then, I'd rotate the machine 20 degrees and do it again. It spread out about fifteen feet – I was set up 30 feet from the house.

About half the yard was done when my daughter walked out of the house, waving wildly and pointing at the floor-to-ceiling window on the east side of the sunroom. Apparently, there was a very small rock in the bag of manure I'd just emptied into the shredder that was thrown a lot further than fifteen feet.

From an artistic point of view, the extensively cracked glass reflecting the sunlight was lovely.

From my husband's point of view, it was expensive.

Of course, my daughter had to call my mom and tell her what happened. My 86-year-old Mother laughed so hard she cried, then proceeded to call all five of my siblings to let them know what happened to Rosie when the shit hit the fan.

Rosie's Favorite Exercise Outfit

Gardening –
The Best Kind of Exercise

The primary care doctor I'd been with for over 20 years retired a couple years ago. This meant hunting around for a new physician on my insurance plan, preferably one who had experience with older patients since I have now entered the exciting arena of senior citizenship. I prefer women physicians, and there was one who was a geriatric specialist with an opening, so I made an appointment for my annual physical.

Upon meeting her, I could tell this Doctor was not a warm fuzzy kind of person, but I figured if she was competent, we could get used to each other. We ran through all the standard questions, and she made the usual comments about me being somewhat overweight. I am used to that.

Then she asked how often I exercised and what kind did I do? I told her I am a Master Gardener and I work in my garden every day the sun shone.

Her response was, "That is NOT exercise!"

Now, I don't know what she thought a gardener meant. She probably thinks gardeners are people who drive up to Walmart or Home Depot and get a couple potted plants, and after putting them in the ground, the only exercise they do is watering.

Boy, is she mistaken!

My half-acre property has two primary garden areas. The front yard is flowers, shade trees, herbs, and some grass. In the back, I have a large vegetable garden, 50x60 feet, with 12 raised beds, six fruit trees, and a 10x20 foot ground set corn bed.

Every time I go outside, I don my fancy exercise outfit: broad-brimmed hat, old jeans and t-shirt, gloves, and sunscreen. Then I choose the day's high-tech exercise equipment: wheelbarrow, bucket, shovel, rake, and a big garden knife.

The raised beds for the vegetable garden were created from a stack of lumber leftover from other projects, and I was gifted with about 24 standard-size straw bales. It is a point of pride for me that I use and reuse what I have on hand rather than go to the store for new stuff.

A couple months back, an acquaintance who lived back east posted a video of herself with her physical fitness trainer running through some of his "special exercise techniques." There was a large tractor tire in the middle of a parking lot, and my friend was lifting it up and pushing it over.

Hmmm. Turning over a tractor tire…and the area she was in was nowhere near a farm by the tall buildings in the background.

Doesn't that seem silly?

When I told her I had a tractor out west here and a ranchette where she could actually do something practical while exercising, she unfriended me on Facebook. Of course, she'd probably need to buy some jeans and cotton shirts instead of the bright pink and black workout clothes that probably cost more than a new goat.

I realize city folks spend all day sitting in cubicles with artificial lighting, so they have to find ways of staying physically in shape to be healthy. Like them, I was stuck in the D.C. area for two years in my job. But I just can't see paying money for the right to use a lot of machines – also indoors under artificial lighting – or having a private coach with "innovative" methods that look a lot like old-fashioned farming.

Working and living for any time at all in the D.C. area was a major attitude adjustment. It was never supposed to take YEARS for me to get back home to the desert, and the East Coast did its best to make me feel unwelcome, starting with the cost of living. Rent on apartments cost more than the mortgage of my place in Albuquerque.

Driving east on I-40 became very exciting when the ice storm hit. Ever see a GMC dually with a Uhaul trailer hit a sheet of ice in the middle of a bridge? I didn't know a one-ton pickup could spin in a complete circle…several times.

I'd only been in that apartment for a month when the east coast was hit by Snowmaggedon. The weather service predicted heavy snow conditions starting Saturday. In a sneaky sort of way, the day began overcast with little white flakes drifting casually to the ground. By 10am the heavy flakes were 8 inches deep.

Excellent! I thought as I pulled out my snow shovel – this was good useful exercise. There wasn't much wind, just lots of snow – so different from the high desert. It was a pleasure to actually stretch my muscles and fantasize how nice it would be if this kind of moisture were touching the New Mexico mountains…the pinon trees and our reservoirs really needed it.

The apartment had a small pull-in area off of the complex parking lot that was part of the package, so I grabbed a snow shovel and went to work. The area was 6 feet wide and 10 feet long. I pushed the shovel across the asphalt then put my back into it as I tossed the heavy slushy piles to the side. When I got to the end I turned back to admire my handiwork, but while my back was turned Mother Nature recovered the entire thing!

Knowing the temperatures were going to drop further that night I trudged out every two hours and scraped another 8-10 inches or more from my parking area. By the time I gave up at midnight the snow surrounding my little valley was even with the top of the GMC's wheel wells.

In 36 hours it snowed over five feet. The parking lot was a solid lumpy blanket of sparkling white…and I'd had enough exercise for a month.

During the next few months I found several state parks that needed help with keeping trails cleaned up or weeding gardens. There was an animal rescue ranch not far away where I could help out and get to ride the horses. I got a lot of exercise one day when the baby pigs got loose.

Every muscle group targeted in a gym is worked thoroughly by anyone who has a yard and garden. Trimming bushes and trees works the forearms, biceps, and hand muscles. Overhead swings with a pickaxe to break up clay soil is good for the abs. Steering a loaded wheelbarrow around clamps the buttocks. Hoeing works the shoulders while shoveling dirt, piles of manure or snow is good for the calves.

The best part is that all this is done outside in the sun. Not a lot of gardeners have vitamin D deficiency. When you get to working on weed whacking the lawn, or mulching the flower beds, you lose track of time because your brain is engaged with details. You don't have to wear a headset while watching TV on your cell phone because running on a treadmill is incredibly boring.

Yards and gardens offer ongoing challenges and the delight of lovely flowers and fresh vegetables.

I have built eleven raised beds out of reclaimed lumber. As each of the veggie beds was built, the bottom was covered in flattened cardboard boxes to help retain water, and PVC pipes were set into the ends to eventually be tied into a watering system.

Twelve of the straw bales are arranged in two squares and filled with composted topsoil. The rest of the bales are lined up and I seasoned them appropriately so they could be direct planted last spring. I have attached some old slightly warped 1x6 inch board to sturdy metal posts at each end. They will provide anchoring for whatever I choose to trellis.

Since I have not had time to make my own compost and buying them by the bag for that large an area would be pricy, I had a local compost creating company called Soilutions deliver a dump truck full to my backyard. That is one huge pile. Some of it was wheelbarrowed to the front yard, and some into the veggie garden.

For my personal exercise program, I spend between two and four hours a day at least 4 times a week in the yard working on this, that and other projects – not bad for 69 years old!

The last time I was in an Master Gardener meeting at the Albuquerque Garden Center, I looked around at the preponderance of older adults and it occurred to me what I was not seeing. There were no walkers, no wheelchairs, and very, few canes. A great many people in this group are my age or older. Obviously, serious gardening is very healthy exercise.

Maybe we should invite physicians to spend time working in our gardens!

***

Chili or Chile?

There is frequently confusion between the words chili and chile – both of which are pronounced the same way.

The favorite crop in the state of New Mexico is a pepper known as the green **chile**. Sometimes this plant is called red chile, but it is basically the same plant with a fruit that is harvested at different times.

Chili describes a spicy stew of Mexican origin containing hot peppers. Frequently the chili contains chiles, or it may contain a number of other spicy peppers all of which are from the genus Capsicum.

You will see both spellings of chile/chili throughout this book as I am a resident of New Mexico. Like the majority of my neighbors, I love the smell of green Chile's roasting in August and am addicted to the flavor of that particular cultivar.

Chaos and Order

Chaos reigns everywhere. Sprigs and leaves spring forth wherever they so desire at the most inconvenient times! Look there! Is that...yes it is...*London Rocket*!!! That demon vector of the curly top virus shelters a bug - the blasted beet leaf hopper. NO NO! IT CANNOT BE ALLOWED TO LIVE!

The great philosophers all theorize that man has a deep inner need to control his environment. In their attempt to bring about order from chaos, our ancient ancestors created mythologies wherein the powers of nature were encapsulated in understandable forms – Apollo represented the sun, Thor's mighty hammer was responsible for the thunderclap, and Love was the gift of Aphrodite.

Yet Earth exists in chaos, a wild, haphazard arrangement of flora, fauna, and weather. Man has an indefinable inner need to tame, mold, and shape that portion of the world with which he or she surrounds themself.

As gardeners, we survey our own small allotments of earth with a critical eye. There is nothing so enticing as a blank slate, yet many times the landscape begins already populated with random foliage not necessarily of our liking. We choose what to keep and what to eradicate.

Is that a nacient Yucca poking tiny spears through the desiccated granite of the Sandia Mountain foothills? It must be saved! Should it remain where it is and all else built around it? Should the footpath at its base be moved a couple feet away so passing dogs and people cannot accidentally despoil it? Or perhaps it would be best to carefully remove it to a spot more aesthetically pleasing?

How shall our own little spot of earth be maintained? My yard is my haven. Should the land around the house provide us with sustenance for the body or for the soul? Can not it give us both? Swiss chard thrusting skyward with cantaloupes at their base, chili peppers dotted about, providing a satisfying display of edible and visual fulfillment.

Native plants are most likely to survive the vagaries of local wind and weather, but does this mean we must forever forbid ourselves the delights of the elusive blueberry or Tropicana canna? Nay, Says I! With rain barrel and emitter, with mulch, hoe, and compost, will I overcome the limitations imposed by my environment!

"TAKE THAT!" I say to bindweed as I dig and pull and spray with vinegar. "BEGONE!" I chop and grasp the goat's head weeds with leather-covered fist, "NO LONGER WILL YOU DISABLE MY LOYAL PETS AS THEY TRANSIT THE YARD!"

As the brilliant colors of a New Mexico Sunset wash over the earth, I sit upon a precisely placed boulder in my yard and delight in the surroundings to which I, the gardener, have brought order.

***

Purslane is a weed for some and food for others. This low ground cover is a succulent that spreads far and fast, creating a very pretty ground cover. But it only lasts from about May to July then gets leggy.

Pluck a strand of the fleshy leaves and chew on them. They have a pleasant neutral flavor that tastes good in salads. Hispanic cultures fry them with onions and peppers.

A New Way to Classify Weeds

Weeds. We pull them, we spray them, we burn them, and vilify their existence in any conversation concerning whatever parcel of land we consider "ours". The interesting thing is that everyone has a different concept of what a weed is. The simplest definition is that a weed is any plant growing in the wrong place or is unwanted.

Living in the high desert means that personal definitions of weeds are radically different than they were where I grew up in Indiana. In city suburban areas where perfect lawns feature identical heights of soft, deep green spears of grass, any anomaly is a blemish on the reputation of the householder. I still remember old Mrs. Banks, who lived across the street, out in her front yard daily on hands and knees with a brown paper grocery bag by her side.

Always perfectly coiffured, she examined every inch of ground and occasionally knelt on a towel to protect her dress. With a weed fork, she savagely bit the ground around the roots of any clover or dandelion, ignorant enough to think they were allowed to germinate in this pristine environment.

Personally, I love spreading clover seed in the yard – it is pretty, and both cold and heat tolerant. If you are lucky, you can spot the occasional four leafed mutation. Keep them for yourself or spread the luck and give them to friends to brighten their day.

Crop plants are rotated in my vegetable garden. This year I planted peppers in a bed that last year produced a bounty of tasty cherry tomatoes. When the first "volunteer" tomato popped up inconveniently amongst the Green Chile's, I carefully transplanted the tender seedling to a more appropriate place where it could send forth verdant branches and luscious little red orbs full of tangy sweet fruit like its progenitor.

A week later, I noticed five more.

What a dilemma! Should I give them ALL appropriate living quarters...or horrors, do I dare say it...KILL THEM!

Apologizing, I pulled them and the dozens of others which followed. To assuage feelings of guilt, I made sure to place their little green carcasses on the compost heap so that I could feel their lives were sacrificed for a greater good.

Plant lovers need to sift through conflicting emotions about whether a plant fits the definition of a weed in their own minds. Within my acre of land, I reign supreme. I consider myself to be a fair and just judge of botanical worth. Therefore, I have created a system whereby I examine each new and unexpected leaf to determine its future.

Tribulus terrestris – aka puncture vine

Does it have thorns or stickers? I do have pyracantha and rosebushes providing a living defense of my property. But ANY plant whose function is not so designated and has the capability to in any way draw blood will not live ten minutes past the first sighting.

Goathead (aka puncturevine) is my mortal enemy, regardless of whether it is my property, or a public playground, or next to the side of a restaurant or coming up through a seam in the sidewalk. Over the years, my pets have suffered enough. I can still see my corgi bouncing in the gate of the doggie relief areas at highway rest stops. She'd yelp and come to a complete halt with one paw in the air. A living statue until I could get to her and remove the painful thorn.

I don't care where I am, if I see those lacey little swirls with tiny yellow flowers – they are history! Luckily the roots are shallow. The plant grows flat along the ground radiating out from the center. You can reach down to the core, which usually doesn't have any stickers, grab and pull. The whole thing comes up at once.

Is it edible? Some weeds are what I call frenemies, like pigweed. A nutritious varietal of amaranth beloved by goats and cattle, pigweed is kinda cute when small, but give them a drop of water, and they become huge bushes overnight with long stringy seed heads containing enough seeds to feed all those starving families in Asia my mom referred to when I would not each spinach as a child.

Clover, grasses, mallow, mullein, and many weeds make good animal feeds – so does milk thistle, which is a frenemy as far as I am concerned because of the stickers.

Young dandelion leaves are tasty in a salad and the dried roots can be brewed into chicory – a coffee-like drink. They can also be fermented into dandelion wine...so it is a weed?

Purslane is another frenemy. This low-spreading vining succulent is delicious in salads and stir-fry. I think it also makes a great ground cover and green manure that shades the roots of taller plants during the harsh heat of summer. It is easy to pull, yet some people don't like that it propagates quickly and generously.

Is it pernicious? When you first see the pretty little flowers on a bindweed vine you might ooohh and ahh and think, "how nice". DO NOT LET IT LIVE! This vining plant snakes its way across the ground and over fences, plants, or any other stationary thing in its path. Within two weeks, bindweed becomes as insidious as an unfounded rumor choking the life out of your innocent green beans and twining wildly up your cornstalks and sunflowers.

Once it is established, it is incredibly hard to get rid of even if you subscribe to the concept that poison is not a totally terrible alternative. The roots go down a couple feet, then spread laterally, and if you don't get every little inch of them out of the ground, they grow into a whole new plant. If you spot even one of its little arrow-shaped leaves, grab a shovel and ATTACK!

Is it poisonous to people or pets? Poison Ivy, oak or sumac are obvious bad guys. But did you know that Texas blue bonnets are toxic? Some salads containing flowers are attractive and tasty. I like the flavor of rose petals, nasturtiums, clover, daylily, and dandelions. However, you need to know which pretty flowers could kill you or your pets if ingested. A few of these are common to household yards, such as narcissus, oleander, periwinkle, and rhododendrons. Datura (blooming nightshade) is a common southwestern roadside vining flower – very pretty and very deadly.

Aesthetics. Is it pretty? Is it ugly? This is the category most subject to personal opinion and the one which most people use to determine the future of any unexpected flora gracing their personal space. Some plants try to sneak their way into a person's good nature by sprouting lovely little flowers.

Example: Devil's claw looks innocent enough when it breaks ground all the way until it is a good two feet tall...the leaves are fuzzy looking and feel like the softer side of Velcro. The flowers are attractive. Once it is established, you better really like it as it creates huge curved woody seedpods that look like...well...claws. At this point, it is a royal pain in the patush to get rid of.

When I see something unfamiliar or different coming up in my garden beds, I usually give it a day or two to figure out if it is a beneficial plant before unilaterally deciding to end its existence. Who knows, it may attract bees or butterflies. It may produce really pretty flowers or provide a stabilizing ground cover.

Plants bring us all joy in many ways, so if you see something unfamiliar in the middle of your petunias, you might take a moment to figure out if it is a new friend or if it meets your personal definition of a weed.

***

Plants CAN Talk!

When you are walking into the garden, do you hear your plants? Do they scream when they are distressed? Do they seem to subtly send out stronger fragrances at times?

Guess what!? YOU ARE NOT CRAZY!

Bona Fide University Laboratory PHD's at two major educational institutions have discovered what gardeners have known for years. Lilach Hadany from Tel Aviv University reports that tomatoes left without water begin making popping noises by the second day – even while the plant still looks good. Their instruments say the popping sound peaks within about five days.

Sounds change depending on the plant and the type/severity of the threat which prompts them, and they differ depending on the plants making them. The sounds happen at the approximate volume of human speech but outside the range of human hearing.

This created a whole new field of study – PLANT ACOUSTICS.

Boy, do I feel vindicated! For years I've walked into areas of the garden, and even though the tree or flower is upright and doesn't look wilty I will tell my husband, "I need to water the gladiolas; they're crying again."

He just gives me this resigned but distinctly unbelieving look and shakes his head.

There's another researcher, Richard Karban, at the University of California Davis who claims that plants can also "hear" and respond to things they hear. He states that primrose bushes can hear the sound of bees buzzing, they then release a stronger fragrance or burst of nectar to entice their allies in the reproduction process.

So, not only do they respond to the "music" of the bees, they also deliberately seduce them. There's always been a lot of hanky panky between insects and flowers, but this brings a whole new level to the Victorian-era art of flower seduction.

From here the researchers are trying to determine the level to which plants hear each other and whether animals can hear plants. If tomatoes cry because they are thirsty, does that warn the other plants nearby to start sealing their cells against dehydration? Are insects more or less likely to lay eggs on a stressed plant?

Apparently the two loudest crybabies discovered so far are tomatoes and tobacco. The tomatoes whine about how they are treated – though if you can't hear them, you can probably taste the flavor difference in a tomato that has been pampered versus one that is stressed.

Tobacco exacts revenge. Think about it - insects know better than to attack tobacco – it kills them. A derivative of tobacco, Nicotine, is a natural insecticide. People wage war on tobacco annually – growing it, then mowing it down, drying, rolling, and burning it for pleasure. Just think, all these years tobacco has been screaming dire threats long before the U.S. Surgeon General required warnings on packs of cigarettes.

Opps, gotta go...my seedlings are calling.

***

Queen of the Compost Holes

"One of these days, I am <u>not</u> going to see one of these, and I will fall in, break my leg, put my back out and YOU will have to be the one handling my bed pan!" Wolf scowled with a twinkle in his eyes as he charmingly berated me.

My husband, Wolf, does have a point, though. That's why I set orange cones and solar lights around the large holes which appear randomly in my yard because I do keep in mind that he has cataracts.

What he was complaining loudly about are my compost holes. I've been to a lot of gardening presentations on compost. It is a very sustainable, organic method of improving soil quality, and since I live in the desert southwest pretty much A-N-Y-T-H-I-N-G organic can help improve the sand/clay combination.

Many years ago, shortly after I'd moved here from the lush verdant fields of Indiana, I visited my friend, Dennis, who had a gift for wood sculpture. We were sitting on his back porch, and I noticed a hole in the ground about four feet away from a big old cottonwood tree. I asked him if he was planning to set something in concrete. A light pole, perhaps? Surely, he wouldn't plant another tree that close to a large older one?

Dennis twixt his lip and told me he was feeding his trees. Then he explained that he does not throw food leftovers or potato peelings or egg shells into the trash can – he digs holes by tree roots and tosses it all in there.

He told me that he would take his vegetable kitchen scraps and drop them in the holes and then add a layer of dirt every week. Every now and then he would get a neighbor to give him some horse manure to add to the hole as well. When the hole was full, he'd top it off with dirt and go dig another one. Eventually, it breaks down into its chemical elements and becomes plant food.

That was the first time I'd heard of "trench composting", though I did not know the term until I read it in Mother Earth News.

What an incredible idea! No more smelly kitchen trash cans, no need for a garbage disposal. Foodstuffs can be grown in the garden, and what is not eaten can be fed back to the earth.

Something similar happened with my front yard garden. With some rough red blocks that I found at Home Depot, I built up an area 24 feet long, 4 feet wide, and 2.5 feet deep against the side and front fences. The next step involved layering about 55 bags of leaves, 4 bags of pine needles, 10 bags of manure, and innumerable little silver bags of coffee grounds, topped off by 4 inches of topsoil. Since this will mostly be landscaped, I also added the litter from my guinea pig cage which is primarily pine shavings, and kitchen compostables.

Over the fall and winter, I watered it as though plants already lived there so as to speed decomposition. Now and then, I took a garden fork and punched in holes, then twisted so as to provide aeration. Much of it already shows promise, with the earthworms having a good time, especially as the days were so warm.

The small live Afghan pine tree we bought to use as a Christmas tree went into the ground first in the southwest corner of the yard. A white lilac graced the southeast corner. A couple Desert Willows grown from seed in my sunroom were next. The yard already contained one Honey Locust tree, and its seeds found the enriched soil delicious. Most of them were pulled up as they made themselves known, but one just happened to choose a location I'd been thinking of putting a tree anyway – so he stayed.

Since that time, I've studied composting and discovered that the earth is seriously voracious. For millennia humans have buried their dead, knowing that eventually, Mother Earth would recycle us all in a practical fashion. (My last Corgi, Honey, is four feet down under the statue of St. Francis in my side yard.) Yet over the past few centuries in this, and other, countries it has been the practice to toss anything and everything we don't want into a trash can and feed it to a magical metal monster toddling down the street once a week.

Abracadabra...no more garbage.

That is, no more garbage in our homes and yards because we are making it someone else's problem.

At some point it seemed ridiculous that while I am throwing away all my nasty food garbage, I am also spending good money to buy organic compost for my flower and vegetable gardens. Something is wrong with this picture.

Several years ago, I created different styles of compost containers for the yard. I made them from straw bales, old garden fencing, wood slats from shipping pallets, large plastic garbage cans, etc... Those worked ok. I would create a new raised bed in the vegetable garden in the fall, line it with cardboard from shipping boxes and fill it with leaves, then toss in kitchen detritus and coffee grounds all winter long. The next spring I topped it with a bit of soil and planted.

Eventually I ran out of places to build new beds in the vegetable garden. what a bummer.

Then I thought about the trees in the front yard and realized I'd been cheating them! The vegetables out back were getting all the benefits of my compost

creativity, while the poor lilacs, desert willows, and Afghan pine subsisted on their annual donation of a garden center vitamin/mineral stake pounded a few feet away from their trunks.

That's when I remembered Dennis's holes. I began by digging one myself – 3 feet deep by about 2 feet wide. This became my go-to repository of kitchen scraps, tea bags, coffee grounds, eggshells, etc. When something smelly went in I tossed some of the dirt piled next to it on top.

When I acquired a half-acre just southeast of Albuquerque, I decided to give it a try in a big way. The soil in the area I planned to garden was very heavy clay. Most of it would eventually have raised beds, but I also wanted to plant fruit and nut trees at some time in the future.

Using a small Kubota backhoe, I dug a couple trenches in the back of the property about 25 feet long. Over the next few weeks, I hauled in 80 bags full of leaves, 10 bags of pine needles, 23 bags of grass clippings, 56 little silver bags full of Starbucks coffee grounds, and about 15 bags full of horse manure from the East Mountain recycling center.

I didn't get too fussy about mixing them all in evenly, just dumped them on top of each other in layers, then used the Kubota to push the soil back on top. Then I waited.

The next spring saw something amazing! The rest of the area contained its usual combination of grasses and desert weeds, but the area I had composted in went wild. It had the same weeds as the rest of the property, but they were HUGE.

At some point I realized that I was being shortsighted about the potential for these voracious cavities. I was not using everything I could be using. Paper and cardboard decompose, so do peanut shells, and pine needles, and corn stalks. When I discovered that fur decomposes, I began grooming the dogs more often. They liked that at first but now they get this panicked look in their eyes when they see me reach for the brush.

Paper towels, napkins, Kleenex, printer paper....when I clean out my file cabinets, I get a little crazy. I used to burn my used checks, but now they disappear into the smelly mix as well. Why bother with shredding old documents when you can soak them and toss them into a hole? Since the trees in the front yard do not produce edible fruits, their holes also make great repositories for animal defecation.

One thing I do NOT toss into these voracious maws are wood ashes. If I lived in the deep south or the far northwestern part of the country where the soil is high in acid, then the wood ash would be a benefit. However, here in the desert southwest, the soil is already very alkaline, so wood ash would do more harm than good.

Compost is the best way to add nutrition to your soil. Almost all vegetable matter can be used as long as it is chopped up enough that it will not simply decide to put down roots in the hole - like bindweed or mint. Manure from herbivores is good, so is chicken manure which is very high in nitrogen. The manure from people and other omnivores or carnivores can be used around trees and plants that are not edible but do not use it for fruit trees. This can contain pathogens which will be transmitted to humans who eat them later.

These days I usually dig a compost hole for the trees every 2 months or so. That's all the time it takes to fill one of these holes since there are only two humans and two dogs in residence. As it gets close to full, I throw some of the original dirt on top, tamp it down, and reach for a shovel.

After the next hole is dug and waiting for fulfillment, I can sit back in the shade of my grateful trees, sipping ice tea and enjoying the wealth of flowers on my wisteria and desert willow.

Petrichor – *noun - a pleasant smell that frequently accompanies the first rain after a long period of warm, dry weather. The smell of water hitting hot, dry soil. (pe͵ trī kôr)*

Petrichor

Heat, dry heat, the soil
Binds all its elements tightly
Enduring torture from
Its distant ally
Which reigns unrestricted
Over the day

I take pity on small
Green things.
Cascading cooling fluid
Across drooping limbs,
And cracked brown
Surfaces.

Gaia's breath exhales
And her skin relaxes
The scent released
Touches my soul
Which then inhales
Her gratitude.

*****

Rio Grande, south of Albuquerque, NM, in 2023

For a few months in 2022 and 2023, the Rio Grande ran dry during a multi-year severe drought. Each year whatever snowfall had graced the northern mountains of New Mexico would melt, and the riverbed flows for a few months. Usually, there is enough rain to at least maintain a shallow flow until midsummer when short heavy rainshowers help bolster waterflow.

An ongoing drought throughout the west has raised concerns as the reservoirs report dwindling supply.

Rio Grande in August of 2020

Water Challenges in Dry Climates

Have you ever read the book *Dune* by Frank Herbert? More likely you've seen one of the movies. The story takes place on a planet completely devoid of lakes, rivers, oceans...pretty much any surface water.

That's what I envisioned when my new boss assigned me to a facility in Albuquerque, New Mexico. Talk about a learning curve! This was quite different from the lush green of the Midwest. Moving to the high desert was a real wake-up call. You MUST water here or things just don't grow.

Greenhorns moving in here (like me) sometimes overcompensate by actually overwatering. Part of the problem is the soil. We don't have beautiful loam, we have sand...water just slides through it back down into the aquafer. You've gotta add compost and other good stuff because plant roots can't grab those water drops fast enough.

The drought conditions we are facing in the western states already have caused city fathers to raise water rates, and they are considering ways to force us to cut back on the amount of water we can use. Obviously, this creates a soul-twisting dilemma for gardeners who love to surround themselves with beautiful flowers or vegetables, but not so for some of the highest water users – the ones who don't give a hoot about long term consequences because come hell or high water (so to speak) they WILL have large, lush lawns!

I was in a hotel in Mesa, Arizona, one bright day in July a couple years ago. It was 1 p.m., and the outdoor temperature was 108 degrees. Behind the hotel was a golf course. This golf course had its sprinklers shooting long, high arcs of water everywhere – watering the grass in the middle of the day.

The huge metropolitan area of Phoenix talks a good game about how they are environmentally friendly because they plant palm trees and encourage xeriscaping, but I saw dozens of fountains throughout the city, little "misters" spraying constantly outside stores to entice customers, and innumerable open "ponds" as part of the landscaping décor. I tried to ask an acquaintance in a gentle manner what they think about this amidst widespread reports of drought drying up the major aquifers, and they flat-out refused to discuss it. Talk about turning a blind eye!

Some towns and cities dictate how many days and what time of day residents are allowed to water. During hot months no one is allowed to water between dawn and evening twilight. If you have a lawn, you must only water specific days of the week. If you leave water on and it runs out of your yard and down the street, you can be fined.

So how do we balance our desires to live in this beautiful area and have some living greenery with the dire predictions of impending disaster?

Individually we can't personally stop climate change, but we can look for advantageous ways to use – or not use – water. Two methods that should become standard in a desert environment include the use of graywater and rainwater harvesting.

Rainwater harvesting is simply gathering the bounty which falls from the sky and using it after the storm clouds have long past or funneling it to where it will do the most good.

The two places that historically get the most rain in New Mexico are Ruidoso and Sandia Park. Both normally get 18-20 inches a year – this is half of what you see in the Midwest and a third of that in the

Deep South. The Phoenix and Albuquerque areas receive an average of 8.8 inches a year. These numbers have been reducing in recent years.

A home rainwater catchment system requires gutters on the house that drain to a storage tank. In an average year in the Albuquerque/Santa Fe areas, you can get five gallons per square foot of roof per year, not all at once of course! A 2050-square-foot home could allow you to collect 10,250 gallons a year. The rain barrel or storage tank should have a spigot near the base that allows you to attach a hose and an overflow valve that allows excess to spill in the most beneficial direction.

In the southwestern desert regions, we have sporadic precipitation in winter and early spring. There are extended dry periods in late spring through early summer and again in late fall. The greatest amount of rainfall occurs in what we call our "monsoon" season – July to mid-September. It is completely dependent upon weather systems from the pacific and in the Gulf of Mexico. If we have a deep low-pressure system, such as a typhoon traveling northeast from the Baja, and a strong high-pressure system stabilized over the Gulf, we get LOTS of rain in a relatively short period of time.

If you have a large piece of property, you can sculpt the landscape so that rainwater naturally flows towards your fruit trees or bushes. The New Mexico State Engineer's office publishes a guide to Rainwater Harvesting that goes into great detail. You can find the info online at: ose.nm.gov.

Another form of water conservation (one that is more reliable) is the use of gray water. It always annoys me that after I take a shower or bath, the water used just flushes away down the drain. I paid for that water! Gray water comes from baths and clothes washers and can be used on non-edible plants or lawns to supplement regular watering. It is especially effective if you use biodegradable non-toxic soaps. Do not collect water containing bleach, and do not use the nasty Black

Water. Black water comes from toilets and kitchen sinks and can contain harmful bacteria and viruses.

Many larger towns and cities in the desert southwest have set up guidelines for watering in the dry months. Santa Barbara County in California publishes a booklet on how to tap into your existing pipes to divert graywater to a surge tank and suggestions for filtration. They recommend that a professional plumber do the work in order to meet local building codes.

One cause for concern in collecting water using either method is the need to make sure the water is used in a timely manner and does not turn stagnant. Stagnation causes mosquito populations to increase dramatically. Not that this happens very often in the desert.

*****

Plant Guilt Trips

Plants are the laziest creatures on the planet – think about it. The current scientific explanation of life on this planet states that everything – plant and animal - began life as single cell organisms wiggling around the primordial ooze. The amoebas which later started swimming, crawling, walking, or flying got organized and energized – they MOVED, they collided, they evolved into various critters that learned and migrated and cooperated.

What did the plant ancestors do? They clumped together and floated until a wave tossed them up on the land. Once on the land they just lay there. The chemical reaction with dirt, rock and sunshine stimulated changes in the basic chemistry so some of them began developing cells. But generally, they are happy just growing, living and dying wherever the seed falls unless a person, or an accommodating animal, transports it elsewhere.

It's the dead of winter and I am watering the yard. Folks who don't live in the desert will be raising their eyebrows, but if you love plants and you force them to live in the desert…I am sure you'll understand why.

Here in the southwestern high desert (over 4,000 feet MSL) the temperature, winter or summer, fluctuates daily by 20 to 30 degrees because thin dry air does not retain daytime heat. As I write this in mid-January it is a delightful 52 degrees Fahrenheit. Last night it was down to 30°F – tonight's forecast is 28°F.

Plants living here go from nice warm and sunny to freezing almost every single day. (New Mexico has an average of FIVE overcast days a year).

Let's compare this to someplace due east of here, but at a lower altitude – say…. Nashville, TN. Right now they are showing it is 68°F degrees, and their forecast low is 61°F …only 7 degrees of difference! Most of the time the moist lowland temps average a diurnal difference of about 10 to 12 degrees max unless a front is on its way. Plants can handle that pretty well.

Plants native to desert conditions understand the temperature swings like Native Americans understand the land as a whole. They thrive on alkaline sand and clay and know how to curl up and play dead between infrequent rainfalls without really succumbing.

Some of the native southwestern plants are edible like prickly pear cactus pads, yucca flowers, purslane, pinion tree nuts. You do have to tussle with thorns and sharp edges to find the edible parts and except for the flowers and purslane they don't taste very good. So, when humanity began inhabiting the desert, we wrestled edible vegetation away from where it was comfortable, plopped it into the alkaline sands and ordered it to grow.

So, I can't blame the plants – be they ornamental or edible – because here I am standing outside in early January giving them a drink. It's inconvenient to hook up the long hose, spray, and then unhook it and make sure it is completely emptied out whenever I do. The big temperature swings are hell on hoses. I do have an underground watering system to the vegetable garden – it was disconnected and the water blown out when temps started dancing down below freezing every night. (Learned my lesson when a pump froze and broke last year)

I can't just water one of them – the others seem to bend ever slightly towards my hands as though straining to absorb any stray vapors. They send out soft pathetic whimpers in waves when they see just one get watered. My German Shepherds could take lessons in begging from the lettuce and sunflowers.

Once the danger of freezing is past the water strategy changes dramatically. The daily temperature swing is quite comfortable in spring and late fall. My underground system delivers just the right amount of water to each tree and raised bed. Spring does bring some really challenging winds – more on that later.

Then comes summer.

Temperatures over a hundred degrees are actually pretty tolerable for people as long as you have some shade. To save on water its always best to water between sunset and sunrise.

What really winds me up is the asinine practice of golf course owners whose inflated self-importance drives them to spray precious water over acres of grass in the middle of a hot afternoon! For heaven's sake – if you are going to play golf in the desert than play it IN THE DESERT!

Make it a more challenging game. Here is the ultimate sand trap, and it is a lot more fun to figure out if what you see is a watering hole or a mirage. Heck, I've seen rattlesnake holes just the right size for golf balls.

You won't find any poison ivy. Instead of forests lining the edges of the fairway you have stands of mesquite and cactus. Makes it a challenge worthy of Olympians!

*****

Sorry for the segway, where was I…oh yes, summer gardening. Yes, I am one of those crazy folks who likes to grow food in the desert. When I got here, I got hold of a rototiller and ran it over the ground in my backyard and planted things the way Dad taught me back in Indiana. Yeah, massive fail.

That was 40 years ago. After a lot of reading, experimenting, and taking the master gardener training I can finally plant a vegetable garden that uses a minimum of water and produces delicious food.

*****

I live half a mile from the Rio Grande. This ongoing drought has not been kind. There's been several weeks over the summer where the river dried up completely, enough that kids on ATVs could be seen tearing up the center. Water is a big concern to the farmers here.

The soil in my yard is about three feet of heavy clay over sand. In order to plant a few fruit and nut trees, we had to use a pickaxe. The displaced clay is set along the base of the fence, and the holes filled with imported dirt, straw and compost. Even so it took a few years of encouragement to get their roots under 'em.

I've built several raised beds for vegetables. To maximize their ability to hold onto water I made them two feet deep then lined the bottom and sides with a few inches of corrugated cardboard before adding dirt and compost. The cardboard acts like a sponge.

Even with water, non-native plants suffer in the sun. Along with the heat they have to deal with solar radiation. Many times, you will see tomatoes, peppers, cucumbers and melons with areas blanched white where exposed to the sun.

If you read packets of tomato and other vegetable seeds you will notice they say "plant in full sun". The people who write that live in Michigan or Maine…NOT New Mexico!

I guess it is good that plants are inherently lazy or they would probably up and move elsewhere after the first 100-degree day. They look so pathetic with their vines and stems leaning down as though trying to hide from the sun. Water doesn't really help with the temps are over 95 degrees – they just sautè faster.

Desert gardeners learn fast that vegetables thrive much better if they have shade for at least a part of the day. I love to experiment with shading options. One of my favorite methods involves 1/2-inch PVC pipes and second-hand gauzy curtains bought from Goodwill.

I affix my 10-foot PVC pipes at each end of the garden box after slipping them through the hemmed edges of the curtains. Reminiscent of a Conestoga wagon, these coverings can be spread over the top completely or gathered to one side. The thin gauze allows enough sunshine through to keep the plants happy while protecting them from the full onslaught. Peppers perk up and the tomatoes sigh with relief.

Other garden beds have trellises shading either the top or one side of the box. The root vegetable beds don't have any covering, but the beets, carrots, onions and garlic are heavily mulched with straw. Cucumbers also love to climb the west side trellis which in turn shades other vegetables in the afternoons. They all seem to cooperate happily when not being overwhelmed by solar radiation.

If you plant something and don't take care of it you will feel guilty when it curls up and dies. I swear I can "hear" them crying when they are dry or hot or freezing cold. (After 30 years of being together, my husband is finally able to hear some of them as well – but only his favorites).

Over the next few pages I will go over several ways to protect plants from too much wind, heat, and solar radiation.

***

The Heat is Coming!
The Heat is Coming!

It is April as I write this missive. Two weeks ago, we had freezing temperatures at night and nice 60–70-degree temperatures during the day. Within a week, we were no longer freezing at night and the daytime highs were in the 80's already. Once again, winter flips to summer in New Mexico with the only noticeable transition being the screaming, raging winds.

Last year a freak, really late and really hard freeze pretty much killed any possibility of a fruit harvest in northern New Mexico. Keep your fingers crossed that this year is not a repeat.

The National Weather Service is concerned with our heat and drought situations. In 2020 there were several weeks of temperatures over 105 degrees and with its last vengeful breath that cursed year denied our lovely mountains more than a whisper of snowpack. The Rio Grande is running low already—not a good sign of things to come.

Anyone wanting to grow their own vegetables and flowers in harsh climates really needs to step back and consider the best ways to protect them from being scorched. First of all, if there is any way possible, give them some shade!

As I wrote in my book *Creating Microclimates for High Desert Gardening*, New Mexico is third in the nation for the amount of solar radiation that strikes our surface, waters, and plants. At this altitude we lack that extra 5,000 to 6,000 feet of atmosphere enjoyed by those closer to sea level.

However, when we notice that certain plants are suffering from sun burn, we can take steps to make them more comfortable—at least until the monsoons offer afternoon cloud cover again on a regular basis.

Remember that the seed packets for many plants and vegetable have information and instructions written by people who live in Michigan or Maine where there is 5,000 feet more atmosphere shielding the surface from excessive sun.

Contrary to what is written on seed packets: TOMATOES AND OTHER PLANTS DO NOT NEED FULL SUN IN HIGHER ELEVATIONS TO GROW.

A lot of the plants here grow quite well on half the recommended hours of direct sunlight or even just on reflected sunlight. My yard has a mixture of garden areas but almost all of the plants are protected from a full day of solar radiation by some kind of shade.

Anyone living in the desert needs to develop water consciousness to ensure that our plants are happy but not overwatered. The most embarrassing thing you can do in a desert neighborhood is to leave the sprinklers on so that water ends up running down a street!

Watering restrictions are in effect right now. On the next page I've listed the official governmental guidance for Bernalillo County, New Mexico, elevation 5,480 feet MSL.

***.

Spray irrigation is NOT allowed between 11am and 7pm from April 1 thru October.

In general, you should only water your yards:
- *Once a week in March*
- *Twice a week in April/May*
- *Three Times a week in June, July, August*
- *Twice a week in September/October*
- *Once a week in November*

Young trees and bushes will benefit if you build the soil up about a foot away from the base to capture water. This basin effect can also be used in flower beds and vegetable gardens to keep water from running off.

So, give your plants a break—protect them from sunburn and water wisely!

***

Garden Water Systems

A way of mitigating overuse of water and still being able to grow your own fruits and vegetables is to set up a point specific irrigation system. THIS IS NOT DIFFICULT! If a 69-year-old lady can figure it out, then YOU can too.

I love PVC pipe – you can play with it like tinker toys. It comes in all kinds of sizes with connectors that change directions and little sprinklers and valves that can be set up on each garden area to deliver exactly as much as the bed or tree needs. There is a special glue that dries in minutes. It comes in two little cans which each have a round fuzzy brush attached to the inside lid. First you use the cleaner – a thin purply blue liquid brushed on the outside of one piece and the inside of another. It kinda makes the PVC soften and cleans off excess dirt and I like the smell. Then you open the other can of clear gel - applying it right on top of the blue stuff. Quickly insert the one into the other with a little twist and hold it tight for 30 seconds.

Voila! You've melded them together tighter than Schwarzenegger's T-shirt.

Be careful though because the only way to get them apart once glued is to cut the pipe and start over.

The hard white PVC pipe is already used in most home construction today. It comes in sizes as large as 8" in diameter and 20 feet long in local hardware stores (those are usually used for sewer lines). If you have a well on the property you may need pieces up to 2 inches in diameter, but if you are planning to hook the system up to the standard household water, you'll only want to go as large as 3/4 inch. That's the size of your exterior house spigots. When you split the water between beds you can easily go down to 1/2-inch pipe.

When setting the system in place permanently between the house and the garden you'll need to dig a ditch down past the frost line and lay it in. PVC will freeze and break if water is left there in the winter. After growing season is past, I get my husband, Wolf, to attach the air compressor from his workshop to my system to blow out the water – it's much less likely to break that way.

If you don't want to tear up walls you can set a connector to the end piece of your garden system to a regular garden hose, just like you do if using a portable sprinkler. Unlike those sprinklers that spew your precious water into the air allowing it to evaporate, the bed specific systems direct water close to the ground.

Even better, there are long, flexible, black plastic tubes to which you can attach plant specific drip tubes and little bitty shower heads.

The pieces/parts are fairly inexpensive and once it is set up you don't have to hand water unless you want to. These pieces can be directly attached to the main PVC line.

If this sounds like something you'd like to try, Home Depot usually has workshops on it a few times a year – check with your local store.

Over the next few pages, I'll provide more info and examples. Go to any hardware store to get PVC pipe. I recommend getting a long stick of ½ inch PVC and talking to one of the experts about options for cutting it. There is a cutter that fits over it, then you tighten it down and spin it around. That is the safest option and they cut well and easily. You can also use a handsaw, or a table saw, and if you're in a bind a freshly sharpened Ginsu cooking knife is good. (Be careful with all these – you really don't want the knife or saws to slip!)

Also buy some of the connectors and take them home to experiment with making structures – it's like using tinker toys! You will find 90 degree elbows, reducer bushings, end stoppers etc.

Do not buy the PVC glue at first – or if you do then don't open it up until you know exactly how you want to create the final structure.

I like to make a diagram on paper, which includes every bend, every end piece, every connector piece and the length of each pipe. Then I can count them all up, and make sure each piece is cut to length.

Take some spare pieces to experiment on using the glue before putting together the final structure. You will want to wear gloves for this.

Besides gardening, you can make some fun stuff with PVC and glue – just remember that if you intend to run water through the final product than you must use the PVC cement pictured on the previous page. If you are going to put some PVC pieces together for an art project then Elmer's glue, nail polish or hot glue guns can work too.

Speaking of hot glue guns, if you piece together a long PVC box you can hot glue sheer curtain material over it and set it over young plants in early spring. It's so lightweight that us old farts can lift it up easily even if it is 10 feet long by 3 feet wide. Put stone or brick weights on the bottom part of the "box" to keep it from blowing away in a strong wind.

You can see it here, protecting the young green chile plants from a late snow.

*****

Dogs, Mates and Watering

"You'd probably be able to reach the whole area if you ran the hose through the center instead of down one side." My husband, Wolf, stood between the two center columns of the front porch looking my direction. I know he was just trying to be helpful, but as usual when it came to the gardens, he was commenting without knowing the big picture.

"I needed to reach the big prickly pear cactus by the front gate." I replied. "It's on the verge of blooming." Cacti normally don't need too much extra water; they grow slow but steady in all but extreme conditions. But this year's buds promised a fabulous explosion of blooms so I figured I'd help it along.

We are an unlikely couple in many ways. In general Wolf hates anything to do with yardwork – he'd much rather be tinkering around with classic cars in the garage, or going to racetracks. But he doesn't mind helping out when I need to haul around bales of hay or occasionally dig out an area for another plant. Personally, I hate the smell of gasoline, and my concept of a great car is a hatchback that reliably gets me from place to place with a large enough rear storage area so the potted plants don't have to be bent during transport.

But we both love dogs, our kids, and each other...so it works.

As I moved around pointing the hose at the birdbath, the tub of mums, and the iris, Wolf looked over at me and made his next, more relevant, comment. "You really like watering plants, don't you?"

I looked over at him like *DUH?*

"Well, you could just turn on the house watering system that you designed and installed just for that purpose but instead you're walking around with the hose."

I chuckled. 'Yup. But doing it this way once a week or so lets me really LOOK at each plant." I didn't bother to mention that while watering I'd also give them each a little pep talk, complimenting them on their growth or the abundance of flowers, or asking why their stalks appeared a bit thinner than usual.

Wolf came up beside me, which meant that I now had him plus two big German Shepards looking at the water gushing from my hose. Masha nosed my hand and I turned the spray a little in her direction so she could drink from it.

"Where'd you put the turtle?" Wolf asked as he stroked his long white beard. We made an interesting looking couple. He sported wizard length white hair and beard, but wore blue jeans and gray t-shirts with racecar logos. In general, I keep my grey hair pixie short, and in my tie-dyed t-shirts I resemble the cheery looking garden gnomes scattered around my yard.

I nodded to the left. "It's by the bathtub."

Like a lot of comfortably off older parents, I pretty much have everything I need, so the kids are always looking for things I might like for holidays and birthdays. They'd all discovered my big weaknesses: solar lights and thick fuzzy socks. Both my flower garden and my vegetable garden look like fairyland at night.

This morning my daughter, Melissa, had sent a Mother's Day gift – a cat-sized statue of a cute turtle painted green with flowers embedded in the plates of its shell. The flowers contained little lights which lit up after dark. The small solar panel cleverly concealed in the back

Wolf moved over to the area of an old bathtub we'd inherited when purchasing the property. Masha plopped down under the Honey Locust tree. King spotted a huge bumblebee and was headed across the yard at breakneck speed.

I yelled at him. "Hey, Dodo Dog! Get back here and leave him alone!"

King stopped short and gave me his "You're no fun" look, but he trotted back a few steps before plopping his fuzzy butt down. He continued to stare at the bee – occasionally glancing my way to see if I was still paying attention.

"What's the big one with the yellow flowers?" Wolf asked.

"It's called Spanish Broom, or Witch's Broom." I responded. I don't know most of the official Latin names for plants, but the nice thing is that the plants don't care if I call them by common names or fancy ones as long as I pay attention to them. "People used to cut and bind the twig like stems into brooms to sweep floors with."

"Look over here." I pointed at the yucca right next to the Broom. It was one of the babies from a plant in my friend Josie's yard – I potted it up and kept it in my sunroom for a couple years, and last year it was big enough to fend for itself so it came outside. A lovely, graceful stalk was reaching up about a foot above the sword-like leaves. "The blooms should be gorgeous in another week."

I felt Wolf come up behind me and wrap his arms around my waist. "You know that's dangerous when I am holding a hose with water spraying out." I mentioned.

He kissed the top of my hair, then said, "I'm not a plant so I figure I'm safe." I smiled as he started back to the front door with the dogs trotting behind.

***

And What About GRASS?

For many desert environmentalists, grass is the ultimate evil. It requires lots of water over large areas to stay alive.

Yet our souls long for that fresh smelling vibrant mat of soft green vegetation – it entices us to remove our shoes and walk or run playfully. What is a city park if it doesn't have grass? How much more attractive is a house for sale if dominated by a large lawn? Who wants to play on a golf course that has no green?

This is a problem in the desert.

My husband, Wolf, put his foot down a long time ago – he MUST have at least a small area of grass. Once, when we lived on the east side of Sandia Mountain, we had a very lush patch of grass that was a 5'x 5' square. He actually had to mow it a couple times a year, but it made him happy and there in the foothills we didn't need to water very often.

Native grasses growing in desert areas are brittle and spiky. Worse, the other naturally occurring plants come equipped with their own self-defense systems. A small sprinkle of rain engenders all kinds of cacti, tumbleweeds, and (horrors!) GOATHEADS!

Die-hard lawn lovers spend more money than people who embrace xeriscaping. The ground has to be prepped by rototilling it and adding a couple inches of composted topsoil. Most residents resort to installing sod which at least stifles some of the native weeds.

Those who try to economize by hand raking and spreading grass seed usually end up with patchy looking yards. Local garden shops look for "drought tolerant" grass seed – yes, they sell "blue grass" but what comes up would not entice a Kentucky race horse to get down and roll around.

For it to remain green it does need watering – and as was mentioned before, the local communities frequently dictate how much and when.

This is one place that loves greywater – human safe soap phosphates nourish plants. If you can rig the drain from your shower or bathtub to a dedicated tank for lawn watering, you can pat yourself on the back for saving water and still having a spot of green for the dogs to roll in!

Water is precious, it is the lifeblood of the planet. Honor it by thinking about how you use it.

Gardening – Cheaper Than Therapy

It wasn't my fault! I know that. My company closed its Albuquerque facility and like hundreds of others I was now forced to look to look for work elsewhere.

Why did I feel guilty? Why did I feel as though if I had done my job just a hair more efficiently maybe the company would have kept the place open?

NOT. Corporate America doesn't work that way.

A couple months before I'd bought an old adobe house, built in 1935, on half an acre in the Albuquerque south valley area. Both house and yard needed major work – but it really had so much potential. The main house is only 1100 sq. ft, but it has a south facing sunroom, a two story garage/workshop out back, a well, and a separate small adobe storage building. When I gazed at the ragged, trashed out mess of a yard, all I could think was that I belonged here in this place and time.

I sat on a large rock off and on for several days. The landscape matched my mood. Then I brought a camping chair outside one afternoon. This was a little more comfortable and gave me a different perspective.

About fourteen Cinder blocks were scattered in the yard. I got up and went to move a few. It occurred to me that I could set them against the base of the wood slat fence, filling in the holes and gaps around the perimeter.

Yes, that was better.

I picked up a few short pieces of rusted barbed wire and a couple flattened drink cups, and tossed them in the trash can on my way indoors.

***

The next day I propped my feet up on an old wire milk crate and looked, really LOOKED, at what was there.

I saw lots of rocks – fairly large ones, mostly between a foot and 16 inches wide. And they were really neat rocks! Some were petrified wood, some are big chunks of lava rock. They come in greens, pinks, and variegated tan/browns. Somebody went to a lot of trouble to collect all these and then just dumped them in a pile in the yard.

Several five foot tall, nine-inch diameter wooden posts, possibly from old power lines, stuck up in odd areas – no idea why. An old tree trunk with dry rot, over 2.5 feet wide, stood directly outside the front door within 10 feet of the house. With small exception there was no organized vegetation, just a few dead pieces of a single grapevine and some goat head weeds which left annoying burrs in my socks.

The soil looked suspiciously like decomposed granite.

I found a big floppy hat and called my best friend, Elaine. Her big strong teenage son, Keith spent an afternoon helping me pull up posts. Like the cement blocks we placed the posts along the base of the fence. A big mound of dirt in the back of the yard was redistributed into raised beds around the perimeter. My neighbor had horses. It took no great effort to get him to give me several wheelbarrows full of manure which I dug into the beds.

After consulting with friends in the area, I purchased some drought tolerant blue grama grass seed. Keith came over with a rototiller. I followed behind him scattering compost and grass seed in the front yard. The need for a comforting green lawn was at war with my desire to be sensitive about water issues in this desert environment, so the grassy portion of the yard was fairly small. I set up a sprinkler system that only watered at night for a limited time.

I managed to roll the bigger rocks into places where they complimented the future flower beds. Then carefully chose plants that combined texture and color with drought tolerance.

After a few weeks, delicate threads of green bravely reached upwards. I sat in my plastic lawn chair thinking it was almost time for the first mowing of my new yard.

I scavenged old 55-gallon plastic drums and cut them in half. Found old bookshelves with solid wood sides at goodwill and laid them down. These raised beds received a combination of my land's soil, manure, and bags of treated dirt. They were planted with a mixture of seeds and spindly little seedlings. Like parts of my soul, uncertain tendrils put forth small leaves to feed and grow strong in the sunlight.

A brave robin eyed me cautiously while hunting worms between the blooms along the fence. The yard was alive with new growth and color. So was I.

The toil and transformation buried my self-doubts, making compost out of manure. I was ready to bloom again. Within a short time I found a job I loved in a company that appreciated me.

The drab ugly yard had somehow sung in harmony with my spirit. By making changes to it, I had shorn myself of despair and rewove my self-esteem, creating a calmer, happier me. I created my space, and it reached back to transform me.

***

Sage, tarragon, rosemary and lavendar grace this lovely garden.

The artichoke plant grows as large as a bush, and if the fruit is not harvested they burst out into big, beautiful purple flowers.

Edible Gardens in Disguise

Most plant lovers prefer to raise flowers, herbs and vegetables anywhere on our property we want to. However, there are neighborhoods with homeowners' associations that stick their noses into our lives and dictate what we can and cannot do with our own property. They seem especially eager to pass judgement on vegetable gardens in the front and side yards.

I am not talking about the really high-priced properties that allow expensive greenhouses for orchids. It just seems ridiculous that a suburban homeowner who revels in the all-encompassing explosion of flavor which emanates throughout your mouth at a freshly plucked cherry tomato is forever denied Nirvana.

There are some strategies a gardener can use which create the illusion of complete compliance with these ridiculous restrictions. Instead of planting bushes like juniper, (pretty but causes a lot of late winter allergies) plant rosemary, lavender, and sage. These make lovely large bushes. Herbs such as oregano, dill, fennel, and tarragon make marvelous border plants, sprinkle a few green onions and garlic in the borders for visual interest. Line the front porch with various leaf lettuces, carrots and beets.

If the house comes with bushes already in place, can you trim the area between them and the house back far enough to plant peppers or pumpkins? Use existing visual barriers favorably, but make sure there is still enough sunlight getting through.

Arguably you can weave the stalks of grapes and berries into a chain link fence or a trellis. Trellises that face the street can be set to mask cucumbers and pole beans. After all, you are just making a privacy shield...right?

Truly lovely garden additions are broccoli and artichokes. After harvesting the first heads of broccoli, leave some of the small ones behind – they produce exquisitely beautiful flowers!

And don't get me started on artichokes...Wow! These take a bit of time to get their roots under them, but the leaves are large fuzzy lacy looking and spread out over three feet from the center stalk. The central stalk shoots upwards and becomes the familiar lumpy green globe that tastes wonderful when boiled in lemon water then dipped in ghee. After the first year it will send up multiple stalks and THAT is what you are waiting for!

You are not going to eat all the artichoke buds anyway so don't even try. Leave it on the plant! It transforms into a large vibrant purple flower – and do not cut that unless you absolutely have to because the next step comes at the end of the summer when it dries out. The whole plant will turn brown and the flowers become brushy. Now you can use these for dried flower arrangements. When you get tired of those arrangements pull out the fuzzies – there are seeds at the base that you can spread anywhere to make MORE artichokes!

This is just the beginning. Decorative cabbage, purple kale, and rainbow swiss chard enhance any yard while simultaneously guaranteeing salads, cole slaw, and a base your favorite stir fry.

Pepper plants not only spice your food but add intrigue to any yard if you select the right varieties, such as Medusa, Wicked, Onyx Red, Tangerine Dream, Aurora and Black Pearl. One outstanding beauty is called Chinese 5 Color Ornamental Pepper.

I admit it is difficult to disguise a tomato, but if it is in a big pot on the back porch it is not really part of the landscape at all. Zucchini looks fabulous in whiskey barrels. Potatoes can be planted in big mounds and since the produce is underground no one will know it's a vegetable anyway.

One of the big secrets to not getting caught is not to make it LOOK like a vegetable garden. This is what the HMO people really hate because they feel that it would reduce the value of all the properties in the neighborhood. Don't place garden plants in long straight lines the way farmers do in a field. Place bird baths and statues in the center of a circular area. Add pretty raised beds with solar lights on the corners.

Corn is a problem. Those tall slender stalks may be too recognizable even from a distance. If you are thinking of taking a page from all those movies which display images of marijuana growing in the bedroom or garage – I do not advise it. Without bees this is one plant that would require hand pollinating and, besides that, corn needs way more sunlight than you can provide without the electric company getting suspicious.

Does the HMO allow trees? Plant apples, pears, or pecans – preferably in a way that blocks the view from the street.

There is a deep inner satisfaction to having nature's grocery store just a few feet away – so obey the rules. Creatively.

***

Purple Cabbage and Lettuce

Marigolds cozy up to squash flowers.

Gardening in Small Places

One of the places I was transferred to required I only stay for a year. I got there in February and the house I rented in El Paso had a small backyard. With permission from the owner, I built a raised garden bed of decorative stone. It was 2.5 feet tall, 20 feet long and 3 feet wide. It took up a significant percentage of the unused space of what was otherwise a barren area. I spent all last winter filling it with leaves, coffee grounds, some dirt and other compostables. Then at the end of February I topped it all with four inches of topsoil.

The El Paso growing season is divided into two parts – Early Spring and Fall. Winter is pretty much a non-event. You plant in late February, harvest in June. July to early august heat (100 to 115 degrees) kills everything dead unless you cover and water it heavily – which you don't want to do because water is at a premium in the desert! As the monsoon sets in during early August things start to cool so you plant again and can harvest in December. Or you "overwinter" by planting in October and harvesting cool season things the next March.

I intensively planted quite a few things in that small space and all of them produced lushly. Some I intended to be permanent residents, such as the small sage plants, lavendar, rosemary, and an artichoke. The first annuals I planted were spinach, arugula, snow peas, beets and carrots. What few cold days we had were no problem for any of them, I was eating spinach and arugula by the end of March and Snow Peas in april. They finished production as the heat set in late May. The beets and carrots I harvested as needed for dinner, and when the heat set in I covered them with a thick layer of compost so they would survive the heat.

At the end of March, I risked disaster by planting three Roma tomatoes plus two Russian Heirloom beefsteaks. The Zogala was huge – about 5 feet tall. The Krasnoder is the smallest tomato I ever had and not a big producer, but he Romas happily thrived.

To discourage bugs, I planted onion sets, parsley, and nasturtiums along the outer edge of the garden. There were three Big Jim Green chiles which got huge, and about 35 Blue Lake Green Beans bush plants that just kept filling my dinner plates over and over.

The summer heat retarded a lot of growth for a month or so, but I'd rigged a shade cloth to keep the sun from blanching the peppers and tomatoes.

I delayed planting corn along the back wall until the monsoon weather pattern began. I wanted the corn to give my small family the option of corn on the cob for dinner for a long time, so starting August 10th I planted about 15 seeds every 10 days – by the 4th of October the tallest was 6 feet and tasseling out, the smallest was 1.5 feet at that point.

Halfway down the garden bed I had two cabbage plants and over the top of these I set a bracket with some one inch mesh wire. That let me shade the cabbages with a climbing cucumber vine.

Sometimes I forget to write down what was planted where. I found a mystery gourd that I saw sprouting and allowed to grow....and grow...and GROW! I finally had to start hacking it back before it took over the world. The leaves are bigger than elephant ears and the big green gourd is one I don't recognize yet. I suspect it will turn out to be a grey Frankenstein gourd like the one that I had bought last Halloween then composted.

Tucked in amongst the rest I tucked basil, savory, oregano, purple shamrocks and marigolds. The high winds did break a couple of Corn Stalks, but all the rest is a riot of green. In another part of the yard I put a large circle of wire fencing where I tossed my compost from February to June and which later played host to a grocery store remnant sweet potato, a cabbage, a zucchini and a couple Moon-and-Stars Melons.

Other than adding more coffee grounds I have not put any amendments into the soil. I hand water only every other day, except when I have new seeds then I water daily for a week. For a while I had some white moths plaguing the cabbages, but they finally gave up the ghost after I started sprinkling cayenne pepper on the leaves; no other pests have manifested a desire to compete for my dinner.

Small spaces can still bring a lot of pleasure!

Rose decided to help her gardens along by hosting some beehives on the property. Notice the snazzy outfit!

Things You Never Knew about Gardeners

People who are passionate about plants and gardening are often thought of as either gentle, old, fuddy-duddies who can't discuss anything but their roses or tomatoes, or nut-jobs who become postal if a kid or pet in any way damages their petunias or steals a watermelon.

Ok...I plead guilty. I bet you didn't know the secret, hidden side of gardeners, but you can usually identify us if you know what to look for. For instance:

The emergency Go-Bag in the trunk of the car includes a trowel, garden gloves, pruners and at least five packets of fast-growing lettuce seeds - just in case we are trapped in a mountainous area with no cell phone service and have to live in a tent until an intrepid forest ranger passes by.

These are stored in a gallon size bucket along with a couple gallon sized ziploc bags – in case we catch sight of a seedling that is begging to be rescued from its uncomfortable place too near a road and set into a less dangerous environment such as our front yards.

We always share our harvest – whether it is fresh cherry tomatoes, jars of freshly canned lima beans, or several baseball bat size zucchinis. Sometimes forcibly.

The number of broad brimmed straw hats in the closet is only exceeded by the T-shirts with cute garden sayings – and all of them are worn until the holes or stains become embarrassing.

From January to April the mailbox is crammed with garden catalogs. After June the catalogs are used to line the bottom of the latest raised bed.

Most gardeners profess loud opposition to the evils of using herbicides and pesticides and claim their gardens are completely organic. You can spot the ones who are paying that philosophy lip service easily. Check the cracks in the pavement seams around the house.

Not all who call themselves gardeners are created equal. Some of them believe every corner of their yard must contain green things that require their personal attention in order to survive. Some of them have one bedroom dedicated to growing cannabis.

None of us have inch long perfectly polished fingernails, or if we make the effort to get fake ones for a special event, at least one falls off within 24 hours.

Lady gardeners are supposed to wear white gloves, white aprons and only grow white roses. They speak with elegant English accents and host garden parties to fund charity events. Isn't that what we see in the movies?

WHAT THE .....!!! Please see my photograph at the end of the book.

In general, suburban gardeners belong to one of two major groups: vegetable growers and flower lovers. Unless you live in the far southwest where a third major category exists: Cacti.

When gardeners meet they all start talking about their favorite plants. The truly passionate ones display their expertise by calling all plants by their Latin names and recite the phylum, genus and families by heart. The rest of us stand around in blank admiration, then turn to the person next to us and ask how they handle aphid infestations.

We love to take pictures of our favorite plants and flowers and celebrate the first blooms of spring by posting them on Facebook, or texting them to long suffering friends. Our computer screen savers are filled with the vibrant colors of roses, lilacs, and desert willows.

If a gardener has to move into an apartment, the deciding factors for which building they will choose include:
- Does it have a large window, balcony or porch facing south?
- Is there a community garden in the neighborhood?
- How far away is the nearest nursery?

Vegetable gardeners have libraries full of cookbooks dedicated to zucchini. Neighbors, friends, and relatives are treated to zucchini cupcakes, cookies, and smoothies. You can buy a special machine to make Zoodles (zucchini noodles) There are recipes for healthy oven baked zucchini chips if you are on a diet, zucchini stir fry, and my favorite, zucchini fritters for breakfast!

***

The Black Thumb

Whenever I travel to visit my daughters, the first place they always want to have a "girls day out" with me is a beauty salon. What's with that?

Ok, so my hair is usually confined in a sweatband or hat and you could grow clover under my fingernails. I do insist that if I am going to have a manicure I simply MUST have a pedicure as well, which always includes an awesome foot massage.

Like a lot of parents, I have children that I deeply love, though they don't always share my dedications or hobbies. That's fair – they are their own persons. One of my daughters does have a few flowers outside her condo that she waters. The other one only likes plants that are dried or plastic and can be set into wreaths.

You'd think that having me for a mother would somehow pass along a smidge of desire for green growing things, but that strand of DNA apparently was not included in the gene swap. I'm pretty sure their dad's mechanical skills trumped my green thumb.

My daughter, Melissa, has a black thumb. I always hoped it was just a healthy brown, but no, this past year she proved it is truly black.

I visited her newly built home in Maricopa, Arizona, in spring. Already the daily temperatures were in the 90's. The small front yard had been xeriscaped by the builders. The large back yard was surrounded by a six-foot cinder block wall but was otherwise bare.

No, I mean B-A-R-E, as in flat adobe clay. Not a speck of green.

When I asked her what she was planning to do with it, she shrugged and so, being the industrious, creative gardener that I am, it was obvious she needed my help. Grass was pretty much out of the question – they get 115 degrees or higher during the summer months and that would take too much water. Her husband said he heard that mint was a good plant – that it would spread like wildfire.

I offered to put in a small garden area in the back so they could experiment and they agreed – probably just to shut me up. The next visit I brought a 5-gallon bucket full of mint roots and iris bulbs pulled from my own garden. Since I drove there, I also had a shovel, a hoe, gloves and a pickaxe tucked in the back of the Lexus.

We visited a nearby hardware store and bought five bags of composted manure and five bags of garden soil, a soaker hose, and some various flower seedlings. After stopping at Starbucks we headed home.

I knew that the best place for her garden was in the shade generated on the north side of her back porch cover – there was more than enough ambient and reflected sunlight in that area to grow anything. She asked for an oval shaped plot. I donned my floppy hat and grabbed the pickax.

Chopping down into the flat baked clay disturbed very little of the surface, but I kept it up until I had created an oval border three inches wide defining the area. Then I went inside to cool down and drink a glass of ice tea...and take a nap until sunset.

At twilight I took up the pickax once again and continued chopping until the first layer had been breached. Then I took her hose and wet the area down well. The next morning my pickax was able to penetrate a good six inches. That was followed by my turning over the dirt with the shovel before the heat drove me indoors.

That evening, I used the rake to pull some of the soil around to the edges to create a lip of this clay-like material. Then I emptied the composted manure into the "bowl" and wet it down before retiring.

On Day three I added the bags of organic gardening dirt, and planted the mint, iris and seedlings. The final touch was to set the soaker hose in a spiral pattern and attach it to the regular garden hose already there. Perfect!

When my daughter returned home from work that evening I proudly displayed the efforts of three days work. The oval was about twelve feet long by eight feet wide and only the few seedlings were showing because everything else were underground. I assured her they would begin showing their beauty within a few weeks as long as she watered them at least every other day. And, look! All she had to do was turn on the spigot right there at the house and turn it off! She didn't even have to lift the hose at all.

She thanked me and praised my efforts and fed me a delicious meal of Carne Adovada burritos. (Did I mention she is a fabulous cook?)

***

For the next couple months, I would get the occasional text with a photo showing when something had broken through and begun to grow. It was green! The iris and mint started to thrive...and so did the weeds.

What the heck! WEEDS – how can a flat adobe desert surrounded by miles upon miles of MORE flat adobe desert even produce weed seeds?

Towards July things got really hot outside – both day and night. Less photos were texted. The last time I visited her I looked into the back yard and saw a big black oval where the garden had been.

Yes, my daughter has a black thumb.

***

When I left.

At my next visit.

The best kind of pay off to a summer of exercise!

Dirt, Sod and Daily Exercise

One house I bought a few years back came with a rock covered, weed filled back yard, and a standard suburban front lawn. Now this just seemed wrong to me from the git go.

I would rather stretch out on the grass to look at the moon, or play with the dog in the privacy of an enclosed back yard.

So last March, when my husband finally decided to put a circular driveway out front, I thought this was the ideal time to change the whole feeling of both yards.

Now, my doctor recently yelled at me (again) about getting more exercise. She is right – winter definitely encourages sloth in gardeners, and exercise for exercise's sake is…well…boring.

As we got estimates from contractors on the new driveway, I told them that instead of carting off perfectly good topsoil and sod, I wanted it piled on the side of the house. That generated a pile of grass and dirt 40 feet long by 7 feet wide by 4 feet tall. This is my exercise program.

Since we had been thinking of this for a while I had done some preliminary prep work last summer – having the teenage son move rock out of some areas, and I quickly finished a sketchy base for the sod. Last Saturday I donned my exercise outfit; hat, jeans, gloves, and sunscreen, and approached the end of the sod pile with my exercise equipment- wheelbarrow, bucket, shovel, rake and a big knife.

I chose my first victim – a patch of sod sitting nicely on top – about 2 feet wide by 4 feet long by 5 inches deep. I couldn't even begin to budge it.

I thought to tip it into the wheelbarrow, but it laughed at me, so with reckless abandon I began cutting. Pushing, pulling grunting and swearing, I eventually got three big pieces into the wheelbarrow – exercising my upper body.

Then I had to wheel it to the other side of the house. The barrow kept wanting to tip over so I was exercising my balance and coordination. On the other side of the house I lifted, pulled and placed each piece – a full body exercise.

As I moved each barrow full, I also scraped the loose dirt into a bucket to go into my raised bed and compost heap after screening – more weight training.

Bigger chunks of clay like dirt were thrown to the side to dry and later be broken and fed through the chipper/shredder.

My first day I exercised about three hours with only short breaks, and was not bored at all. I got in another two hours the next day. I removed maybe two feet off of the end of the pile and used up at least half a tube of Bengay.

My daughter looked at my nescient backyard lawn and told me it looked like a patchwork quilt. I don't care – I'm getting my exercise – and I knew what it would look like by summer!

An Apology

Dear Mrs. Banks,

When I was fourteen years old my family moved into the house across the street from yours. That was fifty years ago, and I am now approaching the age you were when we first met. I remember you were a retired hairdresser, but you had a small beauty parlor set up in your basement where you took care of a few choice customers and friends. Mom convinced me to have you give me my first permanent, which convinced me that I really look horrible in curls.

It was a delightful sort of middle-class suburban neighborhood. Brick houses with big grass yards and families with lots of kids who would run between houses. We had the largest flat space in our back yard so it was the best for football.

As a kid I sometimes sat on the couch in our living room reading or doing homework. Looking out of the big picture window I would occasionally see you across the street in your front yard wearing gloves and a hat. Down on your knees you held a tool to dig out any plant other than grass which had the temerity to take root in your perfectly lush green lawn.

You would walk around with a small bucket, then focus down at the ground. Very slowly, with a frown, you would bend down and pull up something. If it was being stubborn, you carefully lowered your tall, thin frame and kneeled. The forked took stabbed downward and you worked the offending vegetation loose. Then you slowly steadied yourself and stood up to search for your next victim.

I remember wondering why you were taking out the clover and the dandelions...I thought they looked lovely in the yard. (I always loved spotting four leafed clovers in our own yard). Further, it seemed to me in my arrogant youth that if it hurt to get up and down then why didn't you have somebody else to do it for you?

Over the decades I've developed a love for gardening. Like most gardeners I have very specific ideas about what needs to grow where, and what should NOT be allowed to grow in unapproved spaces. For so long I was able to hoist bags of compost or mulch and spread them about myself, reveling in the scent of freshly turned earth and the frustrated joy of dirt under my fingernails as I planted tomatoes and green chile seedlings in the veggie garden.

Down. Up. Lift. Hoe. Plant. Trim. Harvest...who needs a gym membership to keep in shape when you have a garden?

Now that I am closing on my seventh decade, I find that the bags of compost are much heavier than they used to be, and getting up from the ground requires careful focused placement of feet and hands. Even walking up and down the rows for too long causes swelling and pain in arthritic ankles and knees. Even so, every spring I am irresistibly drawn to garden centers and nurseries, and mentally map out where the cucumbers, garlic and beans will be planted this year. Today I picked out a lovely new variety of hibiscus for the front yard.

As I walked a rocky pathway in my side yard, I saw a tuft of London Rocket poking its nasty little head up and veered over to remove the unwanted trespasser. As I bend down my knees and ankles protested, and suddenly I envisioned you leaning down over a weed, and slowly straightening with a grimace. I know what that look means now.

I also know why you continued to work in your garden for as long as you could. It wasn't that you couldn't afford to pay someone else.

It was your way of defying old age as long as possible. You didn't sit in a chair all day and moan about getting old. Aging is part of living. Letting age cripple you spiritually as well as physically is a matter of choice.

Soon enough I will have to cut back on how much gardening I can do. But until then I will dig and water and prune. I'll sit on the ground and run my hands through the grass or pluck a bouquet and fill the birdbath. I'll wear ankle braces and slather Ben Gay on my swollen joints and keep my cane nearby so I can hobble back to the porch.

I saw you so many years ago, Mrs. Banks, but it's taken over fifty years to understand you. Thank you for being an unknowing teacher, whose lesson was planted in the mind of this child as a seed is planted - awaiting just the right time to grow.

Gratefully yours,
Rosie Kern

Raised Garden Bed Repairs

So today I decided to go and work on one of the raised beds in my vegetable garden. It's wood and one side was deteriorating so it was time to shore it up.

1. Remove all the dirt and redistribute around fruit trees.
2. Find lots of tree roots grown up in the bottom third. Had to rip them out.
3. Look through pile of scrap wood for ¾ inch plywood sheets large enough to cut and fit.
4. Find a Sabre saw and extension cord
5. Sabre saw blade (old) broke halfway through and can't find more blades.
6. Found battery powered circular saw to finish the cuts
7. By this time, I am already sore - but there was still about half an hour to go and tomorrow is supposed to be mega windy.
8. Plywood sheet ½ inch too tall. Go back and trim.
9. Look for appropriately sized screws
10. Look for drill with a full charge...the first three did not function because batteries were dead. (This is Wolf's job)
11. Found one.... looked for bits to match the screws. Challenging, but did.
12. Set plywood in place and screwed in.
13. Started caulking...did minimum then gave up.
14. Took really hot bath, 2 extra strength Tylenol, and an hour nap.
15. Woke up realizing I am glad tomorrow will be very windy because I'll need a much longer nap.

Not bad for a 69-year-old lady.
Hopefully, by Friday, I'll be capable of pain-free movement.

Garden Microclimates

Earlier in the book I commented on the fact that many seed packets will contain instructions to "plant in full sun". This is good advice if you live in the northern two thirds of the US, but not in states along the southern border.

Scientists have determined that our world has six types of climate; Tropical, Dry, Temperate, Continental (sometimes called Mesothermal), Polar, and Alpine. Of course, there are hundreds of combinations of these six where more than one climatic influence is at play, and planetary tilt combined with our rotation around the sun engenders seasonal modifications.

Plants which have sprung into existence in one of those climates may not flourish or even live in a different one without modifications to the environment. Climate is defined as the composite or prevailing weather conditions of a region, as temperature, air pressure, humidity, precipitation, sunshine, cloudiness, and winds, throughout the year, averaged over a series of years. It and soil type are probably the two biggest factors in whether or not a plant flourishes.

So how do we give our seedlings a fighting chance for survival if we happen to live in an area where that plant is not native?

The first step is to study your general area to learn the prevailing climate – especially its extremes. Once you have a handle on your regional characteristics, you can start to look over your property for existing microclimates, or look at how to create ones which will best serve the needs of your plants.

A microclimate is an area of weather conditions differing from the prevailing conditions due to terrain, water features, plant life, or manmade structures. Once you realize how these things can modify weather in your yard you can use them to your best advantage.

Currently I live in the high desert – Dry with greater temperature variations from day to night than sea level conditions. Saving water becomes an imperative here so you look at every gardening option with an eye towards meeting the plants needs without wasting water.

Albuquerque at 35 degrees north latitude has some really hot summers, but an elevation of 5000 Feet above sea level modifies the heat levels significantly from other places on the same latitude in the dry southwest. Needles, California at 983 feet on any given day may be 10°C/13°F hotter at the same time of day, and Flagstaff, Arizona at 7,014 feet, will be 6°C/10°F cooler.

My property elevation in the Rio Grande River valley is 4934 feet. The terrain on both sides rises over 6,000 feet within 10 miles. This means my property is hotter and has less precipitation than the terrain on either side. The monsoon season storms frequently produce plant ripping hailstones. The valley does offer a slightly reduced wind factor – though I have measured winds on my property at 44 knots, and in early 2024 we had a 72 knot wind blast through the valley – that's hurricane force!

My passive solar house was built of terreon adobe in 1937. The front faces south, so the southern walls get really hot in summer, but in winter, they capture heat even on cold days. Cactus and Yucca love it, but other plants fry in the summer.

    The south side sunroom, with shelves placed an inch away from the floor to ceiling windows, receives enough light from the lower sun angle which fills the room with enough light that supplemental grow lights are not necessary. This room is not heated, so I line the lowest shelves along the whole length of the room with plastic milk bottles painted black and filled with water to capture daytime heat and release it back into the area at night.

    Looking at my half acre yard you will see six foot wood fencing around the front yard. A lot of plants benefit by being shaded for at least part of the day by the east and west fences and the north side of the fence never gets direct sun, yet the reflected sunlight is more than enough for everything from lilacs and iris to chrysanthemums and lambs ear. It also reduces damages from the high winds.

    The rest of the property is surrounded by wire fencing which does not stop the wind at all. The very back has some shade from big Siberian elm trees growing on an abandoned irrigation canal.

Otherwise, it is just a big open area composed of alternating areas of clay and sand –natural adobe.

Planting fruit and nut trees required digging very wide holes with a pickaxe. After setting the trees in the holes and adding a lot of soil amendments, I surrounded each about 3 feet out with a 6-inch-high barrier to keep water from running off for the first year. In early spring I cover the soil all around the base with white or reflective material to keep the tree roots cold. This inhibits the tree from flowering while there is a chance of frost damage.

Sore muscles from using that pickaxe convinced me that most of my garden should be in raised beds of some kind. The beds I built all have walls at least 6 inches above the soil level, with a taller barrier on the west side to deflect the strong winds.

Some beds are composed of wood or strawbales, some of masonry block, and some are wells of dirt surrounded by straw bales. I also use food grade plastic 55 gallon drums cut in half. One vegetable bed started out as a 4-foot diameter wire cage four feet high and lined with opaque heavy plastic. Initially it was my compost heap, but after the first year I added topsoil and planted directly into it.

These 4'x8' wooden beds orient east to west and have posts on each corner that rise to an upper frame six feet above. The frame is topped with sheer material which filters sunlight while allowing rain to flow through. The added advantage is protection from hail during summer storms.

Six straw bales were set in a square on their sides in September and half filled with shredded leaves, dirt and manure. This sat fallow all winter and early next spring another six inches of dirt was added. The thick wall of straw still rose 6-8 inches above the planting surface. Broccoli, cabbage, spinach and snow peas were protected during nights where temperatures hovered around freezing.

Raised beds and large pots in the desert give you great control over water and soil. This technique in a really wet climate works to keep roots from becoming too saturated. In wetter areas, gardeners will mound up the soil and set seeds in the top of the mounds. In the desert seeds are planted in the valley between the mounded rows so any rainfall will settle closer to the plants roots.

At one time I lived at 7,000 feet on the top of a forested mountain foothill. The only spot with significant sunlight was against the back of our detached garage. I set the metal structure for a summer sunshade against the wall then covered it with two layers of heavy opaque plastic sheeting. Inside, straw bales were set on the inside edges of the plastic to hold them down. Black plastic jugs of water were set inside to absorb daytime heat.

This inexpensive greenhouse allowed me to nurture some seedlings through the early spring and boxes set inside grew lettuce, spinach, a couple tomatoes, peppers and more during the summer months into late fall. The plastic was easy to block open and the surrounding pinion trees blocked high winds. I had no incursions from ambient wildlife either.

My husband doesn't pay attention to plants very much, but he does like Tropicana Cannas – a water loving plant. We had an old bathtub behind the garage when we bought the house, so I dug a large pit and set the tub into it then filled it with dirt leaving the drain hole unblocked. Since this barrier keeps water from running out away from the cannas they are very happy. Stones set artistically around the edge hide the ugly old tub from view.

Creating the best possible growing conditions for non-native plants means understanding your regional weather then finding ways to modify its effects. Remember, tomatoes in the desert love afternoon shade!

***

Cheapskate Garden Protection

There are many meteorological elements which are both beneficial and destructive to plants throughout the world. Plants need sun, but in the desert it can scald. Plants need precipitation, but some summer storms may be accompanied by leaf tearing hail. A bit of a breeze helps strengthen stalks, but our 30 to 50 knot winds can cause major damage!

There are a number of ways to reduce the effects of dramatic climate conditions. I have a given classes on the topic of how to determine best plant placements to minimize many of them. Professionals with large greenhouses can climate control, but if you just have a small personal garden there are options that don't cost an arm and a leg.

One method of extending the growing season or adding shade in the heat of summer is by placing row covers over your outdoor plants. The rolls of fabric produced and sold for this process can get expensive, but there are other more economical options. This is especially good for peppers, tomatoes, lettuces, some squash/melons or other tender leafy plants. It is not recommended for corn and usually not needed for root crops.

Look for lengths of sheer fabrics at yard sales, resale stores, Goodwill and other donation outlets. Full length window sheer curtains are great because they usually have ways of inserting rods already built in. These fabrics will allow sunlight in and keep bugs out. Depending on how you set them up they will last at least one full season.

Whether you use raised beds or set your plants into the ground you can build a structure out of PVC pipe available cheaply from a hardware store like Home Depot that is flexible yet sturdy. I have used two methods for this, a box-like structure or a hoop house effect.

The hoop house is simplest. You need to determine the length and width of your target garden area. Say the area is 4 feet wide by 6 feet long. You will need one 8-foot piece of white 1.5 to 2-inch wide PVC pipe, which you cut into foot-long lengths. Pound these into the ground at the corners and on both long sides of the area evenly, leaving the top 4 inches showing.

Then purchase four - ¾ in inch white PVC pipes that are 8 feet or 10 feet long. These will fit down into the wider PVC pipes and arch up over the bed. You can attach sheer curtains by running an end piece through the end where curtain rods usually fit. Set that at the end most likely to receive windflow. Attach the rest of the curtain over the top of the other hoops with sturdy plastic clips – I found ones at Harbor Freight for a couple bucks each that have lasted several season.

Once you have it up you can choose to sew several panels together or rearrange the drapes as necessary. You can easily move the fabric back and forth along the hoop to let in more light if needed.

Another way to make a shade/hail/wind reduction structure is to buy several lengths of PVC pipe along with corner and other bracketing pieces then use PVC glue to put them together. This is a LOT simpler than it sounds. Once it is together you can take a hot glue gun and attach Pound 1 foot wooden dowels, or pieces of rebar into the ground equilaterally on either side of the row every 2 to 3 feet. Depending on the width of the row, place a 6 to 8 foot piece of ½ inch PVC over one of the dowels then bend it down and place the other side on top of its opposite number. This makes a tunnel which you can cover with plastic or fabric attached with small plastic clamps. Place stones on the sides and ends to keep the wind from blowing it off.

If the National Weather Services forecasts a really hard freeze – one that does not abate during the day - and you are worried about plants which otherwise overwinter well, throw a wet old blanket over the top the evening before. The moisture will freeze and barrier the cold for a few days. When daytime temperatures climb back to normal winter remove the blanket so the cold tolerant plants can still get some sun.

Both of these protections will help with high winds, killer sun/heat, and hail, especially in the spring and early summer. An added bonus is keeping beet leaf hoppers and squash bugs or other destructive insects away. Brassicas will have a longer growing season and lettuces will delay sending up seed stalks longer.

***

Once used as a divider between rooms, this raised bed cover is lightweight plastic squares bonded together. It perfectly fit the bed where I planted cabbages in March.

The plants did very well – even surviving a late freeze.

Cold Frames and Row Covers

The Albuquerque area's High Desert climate differs from our earth's planetary standard in many ways inimical to non-native plants. Plants need sun, but in the high desert it can scald. We need precipitation, but storms may be accompanied by leaf tearing hail. We like a bit of a breeze, but our 30 to 50 knot winds can cause major damage. Winter's 30 to 40 degree diurnal temperature swings mean we can have pleasant days but freezing nights.

There are a number of ways to modify the effects of our dramatic climate. Many home gardeners like to introduce flowers and vegetables native to milder climates into ours. Keeping them flourishing longer is accomplished best by creating microclimates to even out the growing environment.

One simple and fairly inexpensive method to extend the growing season is to set a cold frame or grow box in an area that gets a good deal of sun. Even in the snow these boxes can provide just enough warmth and protection from other weather elements to grow cold tolerant lettuces, onions, garlic, carrots, spinach, and peas. They offer an early start to cabbage, cauliflower, and broccoli seedlings.

Cooking herbs with dense leaf structures such as sage, rosemary, oregano, scallions and thyme do well with this minimal protection, though thinner leafed basil and tarragon do not.

Although commercial versions are available, it is simple to make a box from lumber, a square of strawbales or even an old set of open backed bookshelves. The sides should be at least 10 inches tall and it is laid directly on the ground.

Cover the top with old windows, shower doors, or plexiglass to let heat and light in during the day, and reduce the outflow of heat at night.

Keep a gallon jug painted black and filled with water inside to absorb heat during the day and release it at night. Electric hot rocks or heating pads may be set inside when a more extended freeze is forecast.

The cold frame captures sunlight and efficiently converts it to heat, so if daytime temperatures are expected to be above 70 degrees be prepared to shift the cover, or lift it an inch, allowing excess heat to flow out between the winter hours of 10am to 3pm. You do not want to accidentally cook the plants!

Another option for rows of plants, including flowering ones are row covers. These can be created easily with ½ inch PVC pipe then covered with plastic or fabric. How elaborate they are is up to you.

A Holiday Debacle

A week before Christmas, the National Weather Service began flooding national media with dire predictions of blizzard conditions. Until that point, autumn's touch had steadily, but slowly begun the process of converting green to brown. The daily temperatures lower just enough to grant warning to gardeners that it was time to finish harvesting and prepare irrigation systems to withstand icy weather.

Now a huge, strong low-pressure system was diving down through Canada towards the great plains. As the leading edge strikes warmer air the temperatures drop 40 to 50 degrees within a few hours' time. Understanding how these systems affect local areas helps farmers and home gardeners to cope. The preparation should begin long before the first snowflake touches down.

Gardening as a kid in Indiana was easy. I tossed seeds onto the fertile soil of the Midwest and things just GREW. Seasons are defined by color. Pale green, pinks, lilac and yellows blossom in the random spring showers. Summer - deep yellows, verdant green and humidity are rampant with growth and tornados. Cooler temperatures of autumn transmute trees and fields into wild orange and reds. Winter arrives white and cold over grey browns punctuated by blizzards with snow that cover the windward side of a house.

When my job initially transferred me to the high deserts of New Mexico, that changed...a lot. Water sprinkled on the ground disappears in seconds. I stopped using a blow dryer on my hair after a shower – just comb it in place and walk outside – presto, majick-o – hair is dry.

Landscape colors are very different – a million shades of pink, yellow, brown with incredibly clear turquoise skies. Here I first saw a truly dense Milky Way draped across the black velvet of space.

The first time I went to my daughter's Little League softball game I wore a swimsuit top and shorts. It was a nice late spring day – no clouds, just a bit of breeze. That was the day I learned the real difference of living a mile high. Less atmosphere to inhibit strong solar radiation had me sleeping on ice packs for the next two days. Less oxygen curtailed my ability to play tennis - it took six months before I could play a full set unwinded. No wonder sports teams from the Midwest playing here always lose!

To live here takes one of two things – either a total dependence on society's ability to grow and transport food, shelter and clothing from someplace else, or knowledge of how to adapt. No, I don't make sandals from Yucca leaves or ride burros, but I have learned to love the food, culture and cuisine of the area.

No matter where you live, to be successful as a gardener requires that you develop an understanding of how weather, altitude, soil and terrain combine to produce the best conditions for growing. Most of those who farm or garden have studied the NWS Hardiness Zone maps. In flat land conditions these maps show the boundary lines of eleven temperature zones evenly spaced from Canada to the southern tips of Texas and Florida – colder to warmer. They align with annual first and last recorded frost dates.

The boundaries between zones in the mountains of northern New Mexico become densely packed and change direction wildly. Albuquerque International Airport (aka Sunport) sits at a mile-high elevation. The city ranges from a mere 4,600 feet MSL along the Rio Grande river valley to over 7,800 feet MSL along the western flank of Sandia Mountain (peak elevation 10,300 ft) on the east side. The differences in altitude create four different zones which can change within feet. How can you prepare for that?

The national Master Gardener program was created by the US Department of Agriculture over 50 years ago. USDA has offices in every state. Although anyone can call and ask them questions, they are primarily focused on commercial farms. The general public began calling their local offices with questions about plant problems, creating an intense demand and not enough experts. Back in 1972, a couple retired Ag agents in Seattle began training local gardeners who would pass along information relevant to their communities. Now spread across the nation, the Master Gardener program offers outstanding training by University level experts, and requires its members to volunteer their services in order to keep their status.

We study variations in soil – the black loam of the Midwest, swampy mud of the deep south...all the way to the decomposing granite found at the base of mountains to the sand composition of southwestern deserts. What kinds of pests seek to destroy local trees or cactus? How do you fight weeds without destroying the health of the soil? How do mountains, valleys, lakes, rivers and oceans affect the lands they touch?

I knew this incoming winter storm would track south along the eastern slopes of the Rocky Mountain chain. The mountains impede its effects – so cities on the western flank are somewhat protected, usually getting a few inches of snow and less wind. The eastern side takes the brunt of the weather, though temperatures would still fall dramatically.

Valleys catch the intensely cold "drainage" of a given area – holding onto it longer than areas midway up the slope, so I prepare for that. Some of my outdoor garden beds remain in use all year. Like many southern gardeners I'd replant a few of them with root vegetables in October.

Onions sets and garlic cloves are covered with at least 6 inches of dirt. Beets, carrots and parsnips planted last spring and only pulled when needed for dinner remain in their beds with mounds of straw on top. Over the winter I'll wander out and pull more as needed for the pot roast.

Master Gardener training does not prepare you for everything. I am a great one for experimenting and trying new things, but I don't always realize that there are some things you really need to research before jumping in because failures get expensive, which can severely irritate your spouse.

Apples, pears, cherries and pecan trees, I decided, would be a good addition to the property. I don't have the arrogance to grow citrus at this altitude in my gardens (except for a dwarf lemon tree in the greenhouse). When winter's chill is expected to fall below zero for an extended period I do take some precautions. Normally there are only a few days where the skies actually contain clouds (we have less than 5 overcast days average per year). The lack of cloud cover means any heat gained from solar during the day diminishes rapidly at sunset. All year long there are 30-to-40-degree temperature swings between day and night. This is appreciated by plants and humans during summer when highs are over a hundred, but it means bitter, dry cold on winter nights.

When I bought this place there was an onsite well in addition to the public water system running to the house. HOW EXCITING! I'd never had a well before. Being close to the river, it is only twelve feet deep. With help from our handyman we enclosed a 50x60 foot area at the back of the property and I laid a really long hose to sprinklers in the veggie garden.

Irrigating everything by hand took a lot of time, and using sprinklers in the desert is a huge waste of water.

After a couple years of that, I took my backhoe and dug a trench from the wellhouse out to the garden at the back of the yard. Carefully I laid in PVC pipe to each fruit tree and the raised beds. Every one of them had its own emitters and on/off valves. Now instead of hand watering everything individually I could flip the switch on the pump motor with every garden plot getting just the right amount of water.

Ain't I smart?!!

Cactus Christmas

We observe a Cactus Christmas,
here in New Mexico,
full of wind and sunshine
though a little short on snow.

The tumbleweed stacked snowman
is sprayed all over white
with a red and green sombrero
and sarape draped just right

Abuelita stirs posole
in a big pot on low boil
then she bakes the chicken mole
all day long you see her toil

Holy guacamole!
Squash the avocado pulp,
stir in lemon juice and spices,
add chips then chew and gulp

Green Chile or Red Chile?
Christmas! They exclaim.
Poured over carne adovada
with arroz and frijolés.

Scents of cinnamon and anise
herald cookies - Oh look there!
Who wants some biscochitos?
Little hands wave in the air.

Ferolitos line the driveway,
paper bags are filled with sand.
La natividad glows warmly
with candles lit by hand

Let others eat their turkeys,
and shovel off the snow.
I love my Cactus Christmas
here in New Mexico!

Rosie with her chest high corn on June 29th

Becoming a Master Gardener

As I mentioned earlier, as a child of 10 in Indiana, my Dad taught me how to dig up a small backyard garden and plant some tomatoes and corn. There was nothing he liked better than to sink his false teeth into the first red, ripe, juicy tomato of the season and munch away on fresh corn on the cob. In Indiana you poked the seeds in the ground, added water and they grew. It was easy

Then I moved to New Mexico. Did you know that tomatoes do not like the soil or the water or the heat of Albuquerque? They looked pathetic. I had never really studied gardening, so I really did not understand what the heck was going on, but I did start reading everything I could.

In the course of my investigations, I discovered that the Department of Agriculture (DOA) doesn't just focus on farms and ranches, they also have a program that is aimed at backyard gardening in urban, suburban or rural environments. They call it the Master Gardener (MG) program and it is offered through their County Extension offices in each state.

Not every county offers the program, but in those that do the county extension agent in association with a group of members sets up classes covering a wide range of information related to gardening. In Albuquerque, the classes are held for 10 weeks, 4 hours at a stretch, on Tuesday mornings beginning in January, when there is little one can do in the garden.

Interns learn about general topics such as *Basic Soil Structure*, and topics focused on the local area such as *The Soils of Albuquerque*. (This is where I learned that what I was trying to grow my tomatoes in was in actuality decomposed granite). The classes are taught by experts in each field – usually professors from your state's agricultural university, or the county agents themselves.

Other topics included Plant Pathology, Entomology, Urban Forestry, Microclimates, and Pesticide Safety. Once you get through those, there are some classes that discuss the basics of different kinds of plants, highlighting the ones that work well in the local area. Roses love New Mexico, so do certain kinds of trees and shrubs. We are taught what are the predominate weeds, and which weeds can become vectors for propagating plant diseases.

To create a good vegetable garden, including tomatoes and corn, you have to compost, compost, compost! Regardless of what the seed packages say, tomatoes and several other veggies prefer partial shade to full sun, though the corn doesn't care as long as it has water and compost. An Albuquerque garden is about 5,000 feet closer to the sun than in the midwest. The solar radiation is stronger here, so a little protection is appreciated by plants (and people!).

Fruit and nuts also need some extra help. Pecans, raspberries and blackberries love the New Mexico soils, but blueberries are and will always be an exercise in frustration. Apples, Pears, Peaches, etc will grow here, but are happier in the northern mountains where they do not bloom too early.

There are even classes in Turf selection and management for those who want a spot of grass in the yard. In the Xeriscape class we learn that you can have a lovely garden, you just need to use good judgement when it comes to your plant selections, and include some water saving options such as drip irrigation.

The program does not end with the classes. To become an official Master Gardener, you have to volunteer your time helping others in your area who are experiencing difficulties in their yards. Each county across the nation has different requirements, but here in Bernalillo County (Albuquerque), we are required to spend at least 20 hours a year manning the garden hotlines, plus another 20 hours doing other approved volunteer work.

The Albuquerque Master Gardeners set up tables at local libraries and farmer's markets, teach kids in the classrooms and through creating school gardens, work with ARCA to make lovely gardens in their group homes, and set up exhibits at the State Fair. Some of them go to people's houses to offer advice in landscaping.

The county extension agent uses the MG program as a filter. Most of the agents are overwhelmed with calls, especially in larger communities. Any questions that the Master Gardeners cannot answer or resolve are put through to the county agent.

The hotline and other volunteer duties truly expand your understanding of gardening, and you can end up fielding some really strange questions. Do you know what is the most common problem in gardens in Albuquerque? Overwatering. People think that since it is a high desert climate, that a little water may be good, but more is better. As a result, a lot of them drown their new planted trees.

Some people will bring tree limbs or leaves into the office itself to ask what is wrong with their plant. One young man brought in one blade of grass and asked me what variety it was. Yeah Right. Fortunately, he also brought some digital photos of the grass and the area it was planted in, so I could diagnose why he was having problems growing turf.

At the end of the season, after all the volunteer hours have been fulfilled, the intern earns the right to be called a Master Gardener. Here in Albuquerque, they are given a certificate, a shirt and a nice plastic Master Gardener nametag, which they are encouraged to wear at all MG events.

To keep the title, MG's are required to volunteer at least 40 hours per year and take six of the classes that are held annually. Each person must spend 20 hours on the hotline, which is manned from March through September and is the most important aspect of the program.

To find out if you have access to a Master Gardener program in your area, contact your county agricultural extension offices. You could also Google "Master Gardeners" and your state. Our local website is www.abqmastergardeners.org.

I still keep tomatoes. As I write this article it is the last week in June. My Roma tomatoes are beginning to turn red, and my corn is chest high. Dad would be proud.

Master Gardener Training includes information on bugs, weeds, weather, plants and plant diseases and soil.

Learning Pains

Aka – Just Plain Stupid

Actually, it did work pretty well. Just before the first freeze of the year came along I watered the fruit and nut trees – which helped them balance the temps. This primed the whole irrigation system of course.

Then the freeze hit and we all stayed indoors for a couple days, after which I sauntered outside to the garden enclosure. Horrors! Two of the PVC connections above ground had frozen and cracked.

Luckily the growing season was over that year, but the worst was yet to come. I knew that the underground pipes were probably ok, and the pump at the wellhead was metal – iron and aluminum, so I figured it would be good until spring.

STUPID AWARD NUMBER TWO. An unusually deep and long winter freeze hit in February. When the winds finally died down I ventured forth all bundled up. The greenhouse was doing ok. The snow was a hard crunchy blanket protecting the overwintered veggies. I peeked at the pump by the well head. A jagged crack ran diagonally across the front of the pump sporting a thick line of ice. Yes, folks, that was expensive.

Luckily, my patient husband, Wolf, is big into fixing up old cars. The next year as the temperatures dropped after Thanksgiving, we rigged an attachment that could be screwed into the well head. From there we ran a hose back to his air compressor. I opened all the valves and he let it rip. Water sprayed everywhere. All the lines, hoses, emitters and the well head above the ground were emptied in half an hour. It worked...no cracked pipes that year.

My environmental mania causes me to evaluate everything I bring into the house for re-usability. If plastic milk jugs and laundry detergent jugs come in they have to perform more than one service before they are retired. Once the original contents are used, the jugs are spray painted black and filled with water – then set inside the greenhouse. These and the adobe brick floor and back wall absorb heat during the day, radiating it back into the area at night to keep plants from freezing. Others are placed around the well head as a bulwark against the cold.

The weather service predicts subzero temperatures here for the next few days. Red and green plastic chile pepper lights are twinkling on the front porch, the luminarias glow softly in little paper bags and posole soup scents the air. I won't dare Mother Nature to mess with my garden – I am not THAT stupid, but everything else is as ready as I can make it.

***

Innovative Garden Plant Containers

My husband, Wolf, is always shaking his head at the variety of items I refuse to turn into refuse. From the size of a prescription bottle to old iron bathtubs...it offends my sense of rightness to cast off many items and consign them to trash heaps when they are still useful.

Some of them were just not as pretty as when they were first purchased – like the old cast iron porcelain coated bathtub that was tossed into the back yard to rot because one dime sized area on the porcelain rubbed off.

We are such a throw away society! People want things cheap and disposable – and they don't want to be reminded that plastic is made from oil or that it is hard on the environment. As long as their little space is comfortable who gives a care?

Well, I do.

I don't have the ability or desire to live in the backwoods or out on a farm. My home is just outside the city limits in an older suburban area. When I go to either purchase or dispose of foods, clothes, and other things, I try to think ahead to its long-term usage and disposal. I tend to purchase things that are either recyclable or reusable. Some of the ways they are reused can be quite innovative.

Rarely do I purchase plant containers specifically for that purpose. By the same token, if someone I know is doing a bathroom remodel, I might take note of whether or not the bathtub is being replaced.

***

55 gallon plastic barrels cut in half

Straw bales set in a square and filled with dirt and compost.

Creative Raised Beds

Living in the south valley of Albuquerque, my yard has two kinds of soil – sand and clay. When you add rain the yard rapidly turns to adobe. To garden in this challenging condition required that I find ways to accumulate and contain organic matter and good dirt – in other words I needed to make raised beds.

I won 100 adobe blocks in a raffle at the New Mexico Solar Energy Association's annual Solar Fiesta. By stacking them three deep I was able to artistically enclose half of the decorative plant area in the front yard. The other half was created by stacking large stones to line the area and cover the sides of a bathtub.

Bathtub? Well, yes. Like many old south valley properties mine had some really odd items piled or scattered over the half acre yard. From previous owners I inherited a large solar food dryer, several hundred panes of 36x6 inch glass, a large mound of shredded wood mulch, two bathtubs, and some really interesting big rocks half buried in the front yard. For the first two months I lived there my daily exercise program involved digging these rocks up and moving them into pleasing and useful piles.

Some of the plants I wanted in the front yard prefer to stay moister than our desert climate allows, so I dug out a trench and dropped in a bathtub so only the top five inches could be seen. Then I surrounded it with rocks to hide the edges.

The decorative garden well begun, I turned to the challenge of creating a place for my vegetable garden. I really don't have a lot of money to buy the fancy plastic or wood containers, but I wanted something to hold onto precious moisture instead of letting it run off. Since the veggie garden is not in a publically visible part of the property, I figured I could use something, well, different.

I started with a fairly large round kiddie pool – the hard blue plastic kind you find at Wal-Mart. I'd used it the summer before to bathe the dogs. It was about six feet in diameter and a foot deep. Because I wanted SOME drainage, I poked a few strategic holes in the bottom. This will be a good bed for my green chile peppers surrounded by nasturtiums.

In the big storage building out back was the frame of a king sized waterbed. These are built out of 2x12's because they have to be sturdy enough to contain a few hundred-gallon water bladder. Placing it up against the wire fence makes it perfect for either cucumbers or string beans on one side. Bush beans can be planted on the other three sides with corn in the middle.

Casting my gaze further around the storage area, I found a cabinet about 2 feet deep whose doors had fallen off. Five feet tall, it originally had two shelves on top with three drawers on the bottom half. By removing the shelves and drawers and turning it on its back I had a nice deep bed for my tomatoes. I removed the hardware from the drawers and set them on the ground to become shallow lettuce and spinach beds. I left the floor of the draws in place to help retain some water, though because they are not sealed they will still have drainage.

While driving down my street I noticed a neighbor had set a solid looking but old and scratched wooden bookshelf by the curb. This item was not too hard to stuff in the back of my Suburu, though my 100-pound German Shepard did not like setting in the passenger seat with his head between the dashboard and the windshield – but he survived the 600 feet from there to our driveway at 20mph.

I left the fixed shelves in this latest addition to my garden. They act as dividers between the various root veggies – carrots, beets, and onions, and they enhance the stability of the piece. Smaller 3x3 foot square shipping crates spaced well apart make nice places for squash and pumpkins to spread out.

Because there are only two of us at home I really don't need to produce huge amounts of food, but I like being able to walk outside and grab some garlic, onions and tomatoes for fresh salsa, or nice fat ears of corn for grilling. A used furniture garden has another advantage, if you decide to re-arrange the area it is fairly easy to move.

If function is more important than form in your garden there are many options for turning trash to treasures. The nice part is that with large green plants spilling out over the edges you don't see what they were, you appreciate what they are.

More Raised Bed Gardening

Living in the high desert means much of the natural landscape is composed of heavy clay soil and sand—which together make adobe. Mountainous areas and much of the foothills consists of decomposing granite. One solution to successful gardening is to create a micro-environment with raised garden beds.

Raised beds are set on top of problematic surfaces, then filled with soil and compost friendly to growing flowers or vegetables. Besides a more friendly growing medium, advantages include:

- Beds can be set up anywhere on the property in a design that allows access for garden carts or wheelchairs.
- Beds can be set on a concrete or asphalt drive.
- They can be set near an area with natural shading, or you can build various options for shading from our temperature extremes into the bed itself.
- Beds can be as low as 12-18 inches high, or set 3 feet high with a lip to sit on while you are working.
- You can set up a system to make watering easier including water saving drip irrigation.

Beds can be made out of a plethora of materials including wood planks, brick, concrete block, strawbales or wire cages lines with plastic. You can use ranch style watering tanks, food grade 55 gallon barrels cut in half, children's hard plastic swimming pools an even some stout old furniture. (Water beds make great garden beds.)

Many old entertainment centers and book shelves are constructed of really good solid wood. Just lay them down and remove the shelves. Backing helps to keep the water in the bed so don't remove it.

If you are planning to build vegetable beds from wood, make sure that you do not use pressure treated wood (it contains arsenic), particle board or pressed wood. Plain redwood or pine can be treated with linseed oil on the insides after they are built to help keep the wood from decomposing. The outsides of beds can be painted for decoration, but you don't want paint on the inside where plant roots can pick up chemicals.

With our high summer temperatures, all plants enjoy a break from the heat. Set your raised beds up where they get shade for part of the day—especially from noon to 5pm in the summertime. If there is no natural shade in the area, add a trellis, or partial covering over the beds. You can set blocks on the western edge or poke bamboo poles in the ground on the west side for late afternoon sun. These can also provide blockage from the strong westerly winds.

This is especially true for beds made from metal watering tanks. Without something to block the sun hitting the metal, plants roots may fry!

Taller raised beds are a blessing to people with mobility issues. However, you don't need to fill them completely with expensive garden soil. In the bottom you can stack concrete bricks, rocks, old pieces of wood, or branches and logs. Cover them with fall garden leaves or compost then add composted garden soil to the top 18 inches.

Add a lip to the outside edge which makes leaning in easier. Raised beds are remarkably flexible, so create some that fill YOUR needs!

***

Do you see it?

I'm Looking Over...

I found a four-leaf clover!

There is a narrow seam between the curb and a sidewalk on my street. Strolling home with my small bag of groceries, not doing anything but musing on the day. Then there it was...sticking up above the surrounding weeds a good inch or two and swaying gently in a wisp of breeze. The sun floated above the late afternoon haze, warm enough to banish thoughts of last week's chill.

When I was a child it used to puzzle me as to why my older neighbor would stalk through her yard with a frown, searching for and weeding out anything that was not grass. She held a particular anathema towards clover.

Even as a kid, I loved, and still LOVE clover. All kinds elicit fuzzy, joyful thoughts when I see them. The tall purple flowers on wild clover in fields wave hello in a breeze. Every spring I buy a cardboard can of white clover seed at the garden center and spread it liberally all over the lawn areas—especially around the base of fruit trees. When I learned that clover imbues the soil with nitrogen I was delighted and now you'll find it sprinkled on some flower and vegetable beds as well.

Clover stays green and healthy when grass fades in cold temperatures, and though it casts accusing looks at me if not watered regularly in summer, just giving it a sprinkle makes it bounce up and smile. You can mow the yard and it sends up new leaves within days. Bees love the flowers.

When you find one, for a moment in time, everything seemed brighter and happier, as though this symbol of good fortune says – "don't worry, things will work out.

And it IS lucky! I find four-leaf clovers frequently, and over the years, I've found five, six, and even a couple seven leafed ones. Seeing the odd number of leaves in a large area of three-leafed clovers has always been one of my talents. As a teen, I decided one day to see how many four-leafed clovers I could find in fifteen minutes if I was actually looking for them and came up with 17. At the same time, I found a couple five leafers and a seven leafer!

My Welsh Corgi, Honey, loved to roll in thick patches of clover wherever we traveled. Visiting rest stops, she'd wander around looking for clover, and in finding it, would flip over, and all four paws would wave in the air as she nestled in.

Carefully I snapped the clover stem and carried it back to the small apartment. I found a glass and used the last of a bottle of water so no chlorine would cause it to wither too soon.

The clover floats next to my keyboard, where I can see it. With each glance, I wonder if finding the clover means that good fortune will be coming upon me soon or was the good luck simply finding the clover. Either way, I'm smiling.

In my book, clover is not a weed; it is a beautiful benefactor for our soils and souls.

Soil Sponges

Soil sponges are a way of creating a moisture barrier for raised beds or a subsoil water retention pocket for trees and bushes. Depending on how you create them, they are also methods of recycling and composting!

The basic concept is burying layers of corrugated cardboard or other porous paper-based materials below or around your plants. In my garden, all the raised beds are 20 inches high. The ground level has 5 layers of cardboard gleaned from a friend's kitchen remodel project. (This also acts as a weed barrier.) Then I put in 10 inches of a soil/compost mix, covered by two more layers of cardboard, then fill the rest with topsoil.

If you have large trees already in the ground, dig 3-foot-deep holes about 3 to 4 feet away from the trunk, being careful not to cut any major roots. They should be at least 18 inches to 2 feet wide. Smaller trees or transplants can have them closer. You simply roll and bury corrugated cardboard (paper grocery sacks work well too). I like to open the hole and set the cardboard in place but hold off on filling it in. Do water it thoroughly right away, though.

Over the next couple weeks, I add kitchen compost to the hole—each layer followed by a couple inches of dirt until it is filled. This enriches the soil as well as adding water retention. When that is filled, I dig another one on the other side of the tree.

If you are landscaping and setting up a long ground set area for the garden, have someone dig a trench the length of the future garden 12-18 inches in depth. Line it with corrugated cardboard and refill it with the topsoil mixed with compost. If your transplant goes deeper than the cardboard, just dig through it and add a few layers below the plant's roots for a very happy garden.

Foresight and Solutions

It's February, and for the first time in a long time, the temperatures are a nice 50 to 60 degrees here in Albuquerque. The screaming winds of spring are supposed to get here starting tomorrow along with some lower temps, but right now the air is gentle on my cheek and the normally razor like shafts of sunlight are tempered by a thin, soft overcast.

I hate it and I love it.

Days like this are so deceptive. Although the seed companies have sent lots of catalogs to entice me during the depressingly cold months I have managed to resist their allure. Mind you, the vast majority of them are from states like Maine, Indiana and South Carolina. The plants they raise, whose vibrant colors and lush sensuous leaves reach out to the imagination from the covers of their catalogs, are accustomed to growing in an environment that is perfect for them.

Seeds from those parent plants have never struggled to find a whisper of moisture in the soil or the air. Where I grew up in Indiana, people would laugh if I told them that they really needed to erect some kind of shade structure for their tomatoes, peppers and leaf lettuces. The first time I walked outside here in New Mexico after a day of over 100 degree weather with clear skies and saw what would have been a truly lovely pimento blanched white on one side – it was heartbreaking.

I had to learn the hard way that where something is planted makes a difference in whether or not it thrives. For the first few years of living in New Mexico starting in 1991, I kept trying to just till the ground in my backyard and planting things there. When they looked pathetic, I added water. But no amount of water alone added to poor soil that is tough to break up is going to encourage lush foliage.

For that to happen, I had to go out and purchase bags of topsoil, and for a while, Miracle Gro was my best Buddy. I saw a magazine, Mother Earth News on the wall in Double Rainbow restaurant. They were kept for customers to peruse and purchase. The concepts and insights were new to me...so I got a subscription to it, then later to Countryside, and later to Backwoods home ... to be honest, I went a little nuts on the topic.

An article by someone in Seattle advocated adding fireplace ashes to the garden...which apparently works in areas where soil is very acidic. It did not help my tomatoes one little bit and the lettuce wouldn't even sprout.

Another article recommended adding a thick layer of straw to keep down the weeds. So, I got a bale from a local feed store, but being a city girl I didn't know the difference between straw and hay. Did you know that hay has a lot of seeds? There was pigweed everywhere! Some of the seeds must have blown over the block wall behind my house because my neighbor complained he'd been pulling it out by the handful as well. (He was a grumpy sort. When I put in a pretty little shed painted a Santa Fe Sand tone on my side of the wall he complained that he thought it was ugly. Yet he had a two story garage that backed up to the same wall further down with putrid yellow strips of paint hanging off!)

About that time I read of a program called "Master Gardeners" which was initiated by the US Department of Agriculture in 1973. It trains volunteers in the science and arts of gardening, who then use their training to help others in their local communities. I found out it was administered in a partnership between a local agricultural university and the county agricultural extension offices in each state.

And there was a very active chapter in Bernalillo County! I really wanted to get into the classes but couldn't for the first few years because they did all their training during my work week. But eventually I was able to move my shifts so I could spend my Tuesday mornings during the first four months of the year at the Albuquerque Garden Center.

Reveling in new knowledge while surrounded by a hundred people equally buoyed with enthusiasm for growing stimulated me to new heights of sheer lunacy when it came to my home and garden. I must have spent $500 that spring at the local plant nursery.

Suddenly I knew WHY some things worked and others failed. I found out that there are 7 different soil types within Bernalillo County alone. If you live within a mile or two of the Rio Grande, your soil is either sand or clay or an adobe-like combination of both.

If you in the far northeast part of Albuquerque up in the foothills of Sandia Mountain then you primarily have decomposed granite - well draining, course and quite infertile.

Between those areas runs spotty areas of both plus a lot of caliche – rubbery clay like strings or patches of a natural concrete made of calcium carbonate.

West of the river the landscape rises towards the bases of seven dormant volcanoes so the soil is simply windblown sand and volcanic rock.

Soils on the east side of the mountain have more organic materials but they barely cover the granite base until you get at least ten miles to the east.

What's a gardener to do?

My job bounced me in and out of Albuquerque several times in ensuing years so I had the opportunity to live in most of those locations for a year or two at a time. Each time I was back I tried to raise my own delicious vegetables – and became more aware of the specific combinations of place affected my plants.

When I moved into a small cedar cabin on the eastern face of Sandia mountain I figured the heat problem would go away. It did. At 7,500 feet elevation in the tall pines and pinion trees the air was fragrant and summers easily tolerable. But it was still the desert...high desert. Desert has a lot more to do with airborne humidity than anything else, so when fire season rolled around we just prayed that those idiots traveling along I-40 would use the ashtray in the car and not flick their butts out the window!

More than once did we hear a fire had started just off the highway and the afternoon winds were whipping it up to dangerous levels. We developed a plan for evacuation it started moving north. I started looking critically at the trees around the house and we cut down any bushes within five feet of the cabin walls.

The soil there was fairly rich, but thin. With granite only a few bare inches down the only way to grow ANYTHING was in raised beds or pots. I was considering some more extensive options when the job took me out of town again.

When I came back I found half an acre just south of Albuquerque that sits within a half mile of the Rio Grande river. It was built back in 1935 and originally was a simple small adobe structure that over time accumulated several additions. The design of the home lends itself well to using passive solar heating and cooling methods so my electric bill is really low.

The soil is primarily clay and sand, but thanks to the Master Gardener training I have had great success. My vegetable garden is about 80% raised beds. The front yard has a small bit of grass that struggles to exist. (My husband, Wolf, and my dogs really like to sit on it.) I have built up a border around it where I experiment with different kinds of ornamental bushes, bulbs, and trees.

The front yard is surrounded by a wood slat fence which offers the border plants a modicum of shade during the really hot months and protection from the 50 mph winds that rip through each spring carrying desert sand. It's also a great place for solar cooking.

The house has a long narrow sunroom along the south side. The glass windows running floor to ceiling allow winter sun to stream in. It strikes the brick floor and adobe wall during the days during winter creating a heat sink. Even on days when it is freezing outside, I can warm the house with a few well-placed fans as long as the sun is shining.

It is February and the sunroom has a cherry tomato plant that extends upwards 8 feet – brushing the ceiling! Planted last November, the fruits are plentiful and just turning red. The window boxes boast leaf lettuce, spinach, chives, green onions, basil and tarragon. Spears of Snake plant aka Sword plant, are crowding out of their planters, the HUGE aloe plant is blooming and the Jade plant really needs cutting back...again.

I'm gazing lustfully at these catalogs, which will probably find their way soon to the recycle bin because I KNOW that the things which have the best chance of growing successfully here are from locally owned nurseries...and I do NOT mean Home Depot. I go there to get pieces and parts for my watering system - but for plants, I go to Rehm's, Agra Greenhouse, Plants of the Southwest, or Plant World in Albuquerque and I order seeds from Sandia Seed.

Passion is a big part of why we garden. Knowledge is how we succeed.

***

Gads Zukes!

Like most gardeners I have a love/hate relationship going on with Zucchini.
- Do I like to eat them? Yes.
- Are they a big showy beautiful plant? Yes
- Are the seeds easy to plant and germinate? Yes
- Do they produce lots of fruit? Oh, yes!
- Do you need any special soil? Not really, zukes grow in almost any media including sandy clay.
- Do they need lots of water? Not any more than the tomatoes or other edible veggies.

So, you say, what's the problem?

There are only two really but these two all by themselves cause a person can drive a person to insanity. The first is the dreaded SQUASH BUGS!!!

Those pernicious critters can find your zucchini faster than the spring wind finds New Mexico. I've read all kinds of advice on prevention from surrounding the core of the plant with smelly distractors like coffee grounds and interplanting with garlic or marigolds, to scattering diatomaceous earth on the soil and leaves. (Organic solutions only: I refuse to support the concept of poisons in my garden).

Those delay discovery by the diabolically fertile mini-monstrosities, but eventually one day you pull aside a huge leaf to find two or more in coital euphoria and clumps of shiny little brown eggs hiding beneath.

However, my biggest dilemma when it comes to zucchini is also the plant's biggest asset – its wonderfully abundant fruit. I love the flavor and flexibility of zucchini. Chunk it up for salads or stir-fries. Slice it lengthwise into boats for baking, shred it for fritters, bread, cakes, or quiche. The list goes on and on.

Even when they successfully hide under the large leaves (which they are famous for) until they are large enough for Mickey Mantle to hit a homer in the world series, you can cut them into chunks for Green Chile Stew!

The problem is that in a household of only two senior citizens (one of whom hates zucchini) ...how many zukes should be planted from a standard packet of seeds?

If you only plant one, it might be a dud. I usually plant three seeds in a mound figuring that if all three grow I can always remove the smallest two. But then I see those lovely little green baby plants struggling upwards and I tend to cave in and let all three achieve maturity. I coo at the first yellow flowers as they open to the ministrations of the local bees.

Almost overnight the first finger sized fruit pops up. Knowing there will be many more I pick them young and start chowing down. By the next week there are several at least 8 inches long and I am trading them to the neighbor across the street for eggs from her chickens or handing them across the fence to the unsuspecting teenager to give to her mom.

By the next week the neighbors were hiding from me, so I took a grocery sack full down to the Joy Junction homeless shelter kitchen. (I also added some tomatoes, garlic and onions so they wouldn't glare at me too much.)

By week four of the harvest I'd shredded and frozen enough to last the winter. I'd also baked and frozen anything I enjoyed combining it with – scallion fritters, zucchini bread, and quiche primarily.

Before then I'd killed a few squash bugs, but I missed my bug patrol for two days and this morning I pulled aside a leaf and ... yep. Armageddon. I figured my only recourse was to quickly and mercilessly destroy them and their favorite habitat.

Donning my garden gloves, I grabbed a large heavy duty trash bag (No way were those suckers going into my compost heap) and squared off against the foe. Bending back the fronds I bent into the center and firmly grasping the base of the plant I HEAVED!

I ended up on my ass covered in dirt, plant and very confused squash bugs. As quickly as my old body could twist I slammed the plant into the trash bag then stood up and did the jittery dance before reaching for the second victim.

Growing season is only half done – but I think that if I get a hankering for fresh zucchini, instead of a second planting I'll just visit the farmer's market.

***

The Fabulous Flavors of Sunshine

There is a star located only 93 million miles away from Earth. Humans simply call it the sun, and we often take it for granted. It rises over the edge of our horizon, crosses the sky, and slides below the opposite side. It does this every day for most of us – unless you live above the Arctic Circle. As a species we know we cannot exist without its light and warmth. It is a blessing we take for granted.

I grew up in the middle-class suburban neighborhood south of Indianapolis where gas or electricity were requirements for heating, cooling, cleaning and cooking. Every summer the TV news folks would choose a very hot day to go downtown, spread aluminum foil on the County Courthouse steps and crack an egg onto it. They then proceeded to tell jokes about how hot it was. I don't ever remember the egg getting completely cooked–but the image stayed with me.

45 years later, I am outside in the garden planting garlic and onion sets while my turkey is browning in a black box cooker sitting on the ground - in late February.

Earlier in this book, I mentioned that my front yard is perfect for solar cooking. "What's that?" You say. Well, glad you asked!

Solar cooking is literally using sunlight to make meals. Imagine eating delicious, full-flavored tasty warm meals that never felt the flicker of a gas flame, electric heating coils, or uneven microwave radiation. Hot meals, baked goods, and snacks that do not add to your utility bill or heat up your home during the summer – which only forces the air conditioning to work harder.

It was a couple decades later when I accompanied my friend, Elaine, to a house where members of the New Mexico Solar Energy Association were meeting. I heard a lot of unfamiliar terms like "photovoltaic" and concepts like sustainable green building techniques. But what I remember the most was my first sight of a solar box cooker.

The Sun Oven was built as a black cube about 18 inches in each direction, with a glass top and aluminum panels that opened out like a flower. There was a dark brown casserole pot inside and tantalizing smells drifting out. It was sitting to the side of the back porch, aimed generally south. The homeowner said he was cooking a pot roast for dinner.

HOLY MACKERALDARANDY! Cooking a pot roast? There were no electric lines leading from the box and no propane tanks attached. Was it safe to eat something cooked like that?!!

Elaine pointed at the thermostat set up against the glass lid – it read 325 degrees!

I had to have one. I love cooking and canning, but this was something completely new. I searched for cookbooks that could tell me more, but there was nothing in any bookstore locally. Scanning my Mother Earth News ads I found one for a booklet on how to build a solar oven which I bought. It contained a few easy recipes, but nothing really extensive or challenging. (yes, we are talking 1990's)

Not having the time, training or resources to build my own, I bought one of the nicely built portable box cookers from Sun Ovens International. This unit was big enough to cook dinner. I also liked that this company used profits from ovens sold in the U.S. to send ovens to third-world countries where people struggle to simply find fuel with which to cook anything. Their solar cooker came with a small booklet of recipes. Other than that I was on my own.

I looked for information about solar cooking, as this was something I could control in my own life. Books I found about solar cooking were mostly about how to build your own oven – they contained very few real recipes to give me an idea on what could be cooked, how to figure out when are the best times of day or year, and whether you need full sunlight all the time. With a bit of preplanning, I could cook anything in a solar oven that I could in a conventional oven. The biggest challenges are wind and clouds.

This simple device forever changed my views of cooking and how little things can make a huge difference in our world. In 1983 I was uprooted from the Midwest. The government stationed me in Albuquerque, New Mexico. Knowing nothing about the southwest I cracked open an atlas (no such thing as google in those days) and discovered I would be moving to the high desert. OMG! I thought I would be living in sand dunes without trees or any plants but cactus.

What a delight and surprise to discover the amazing beauty and variety which inspired someone to call it the "Land of Enchantment". The newspapers had an ad for a solar event in Kit Carson Park up in Taos where I learned more about the New Mexico Solar Energy Association and the many benefits to solar living.

Beginning simply with stews, chili, pot roasts, and cookies, I took notes about what times of day worked the best and how long it took. These ovens come with a built-in thermometer which helps to determine if critical temperatures for various recipes could be reached. By *critical* I am referring to health – not whether the oven achieved temperatures required in cookbooks.

That is one of the key elements to solar cooking – you can cook many foods at a lower temperature for a longer time period and still have a thoroughly cooked, safe meal. However, you must also be aware which things absolutely require higher temperatures to eliminate the possibility of illness, such as eggs and meat dishes.

It's nice that using a sun oven outdoors during hot summer months allows delicious meals without heating up the house – thereby saving on my cooling costs. This is a true benefit living in the Southwest where summers are long and hot. There is also the fact that it's just plain fun and the food tastes wonderful.

My job as an Air Traffic Control Specialist required that I have certification from the National Weather Service (NWS) in order to advise pilots of what airborne flight conditions they can expect. Because of this I'd always been fascinated by cloud types and movement, and I had access to current and forecast wind data – which today is available to anyone wanting to look ahead.

Clear skies bring the highest temperatures in a solar oven. If you are using one that has good insulation it will retain the heat for awhile even if a cloud temporarily blocks sunlight. A high thin cirriform cloud layer does not inhibit solar radiation much, and you can still use the oven if less than 20% of the sky is covered by denser fluffy clouds.

Exterior temperatures are not as big a factor as sunlight in a properly built oven. On a clear day I once cooked Christmas dinner – a small turkey, baked potatoes and a green bean casserole – while living at 7,400 feet MSL with snow on the ground.

Other considerations are: the time of year, your location on the planet, and the local climate expectations. These are relevant to sun angles and how often you can depend on being able to cook anything at all. Where I live in the high desert of northern New Mexico we average only six totally overcast days a year. Even during monsoon season, you can normally expect clear skies during the morning until about 2 pm when the scattered cumulus begin to form.

I've learned to dry fruits and veggies as well with one, or make jerky. There is nothing like growing your own organic food and cooking it with sunlight. The first time you bite into a solar cooked chocolate chip cookie you are totally hooked on the concept.

Socializing with other enthusiasts gave me more ideas for recipes and other uses for the sun's light as it relates to food. Water purification – especially in areas affected by disasters can be critical. A pot of water in a solar oven can distill water as well as cook foods.

I collected recipes from other solar chefs and created a cook book entitled *The Solar Chef*, which is now in its 8th edition and has been read all over the world. This book is unique as it offers insights into the myriad aspects of cooking with sunlight and contained a wide variety of recipes. The book was received enthusiastically by the sustainable living community in general. It received one national and two local book awards and was purchased in bulk by Sun Ovens International for over a decade. It has been updated eight times – the most recent contain gluten free and vegan options.

The beauty of it is that you don't have to live in the desert to do this. The biggest solar cooking museum in the country is located in Minnesota! I cooked my Christmas dinner on the porch behind the house located at 7,300 feet on Sandia Mountain – with six inches of snow on the ground. As long as the sun is out you can cook.

One year I was demonstrating solar cooking at the New Mexico Solar Energy Association's annual Solar Fiesta and was approached by a lady from Florida. She'd read about the event online and traveled to meet me because after Hurricane Andrew had ravaged the state she'd been without power, gas or clean water for over a week. She bought a Sunoven and my cookbook, and I gave her pointers on purifying water.

Today there are a lot of other solar cooking options and informational websites including mine - www.solarranch.com. If you click on the Post about Solar Food Dehydration you get a pretty nice PowerPoint that includes some quirky options for preserving food.

The best part of solar cooking is the flavor, you can taste the sun's blessing in every bite.

Becoming a Solar Chef

Solar Cookers have made a splash all over the world in the last 10 years. In many countries of Africa, there are villages that have little in the way of firewood for cooking; Sun Cookers International is a non-profit group that raises money to bring Sun Ovens made from foil-covered cardboard with oven roasting bags to these areas. A pot of rice and beans placed into this arrangement will cook food for the family without the women having to spend hours searching for a few small sticks of firewood or dried dung.

There is a town just outside Mexico City where the women's association has built a large solar oven. **Panadaria Solaria** is the name of their bakery, which supplies most of the village's bread.

A simple solar oven is made from lining a shoebox with aluminum. Paint the outside of a quart canning jar black. You can put hotdogs or water or anything that needs warmed inside the jar. Place the jar inside the box and tilt it towards the sun. On a sunny day, it should only take 15 to 20 minutes for it to be ready.

There are many plans for building oven sized solar cookers from cardboard or wood, and there are several kinds of solar cookers that are considered to be serious appliances.

The All-American Sun Oven is one such appliance. It has petal-like reflectors and tempered glass doors. It can reach 425 degrees in summer, and even in winter will cook food– as long as there is sun! The beauty of this one is that it folds up quickly, weighs only 21 pounds and is easily transportable. It can be used during camping when the forest service won't even allow camp stoves.

It contains a temperature gauge and a suspended platform that keeps food upright even when the box is tilted to gather maximum sunlight.

There are also several parabolic cookers – curved surfaces that reflect light toward a pot suspended at the point where the light is focused. These can achieve higher temperature and are very good for frying. They usually are not as easily portable as the box cookers, but do very well at boiling the morning coffee!

Although most of us in the United States don't have the problems faced by the women in Africa, there are several advantages in using Solar Cookers in the sunny Southwest. It reduces the amount of gas or electricity we use with regular stoves – lowering the utility bill. It reduces the amount of heat we generate when using conventional stoves indoors – so our air conditioning does not have to blow out the heat – again reducing the utility bills.

There are subtle and important differences between a solar oven and the electric or gas ovens we find in most kitchens. One involves the temperature fluctuation during cooking. This is especially important at lower temps (<300F). The temp fluctuation in a standard oven is dictated by the thermostat deadband, which is normally 40F. That is a big swing from high to low end. (280F to 320F when oven is set at 300F). The solar oven can maintain a more constant level depending on the amount of attention you pay.

Another difference is the source of heat. A standard oven's source is generated at the bottom of the oven. The Solar Oven fully surrounds the food, which is why you do not end up with food that is burned on the bottom.

The disadvantages of a solar oven is that it takes more time and is weather dependent. But this means that the slow cooking enhances the flavors.

There is also the fact that it's just plain fun, and the food tastes wonderful. I bake chocolate chip cookies in mine, or pizza, or just about anything else I want.

You can also treat it like a crockpot. Take something frozen and put it in a clear casserole dish. Set the dish into the solar oven before leaving for work in the morning and point it towards where the sun will be at around 1 pm. When you come home from work a couple of hours later, the casserole is thawed, cooked, and tasty!

The question asked the most by people who have cooked with standard convection ovens in their homes all their lives is "How do you regulate the temperature?" I smile as I turn the oven partially away from the sun and say "warm," then turn it back to face the sun fully and say "hot".

Over time you will acquire a feeling for when the cloud cover is simply too dense to cook in. Just remember, the more clouds, the slower the cook time. This may not affect the soups and all-day dishes very much, but the breads, eggs, and desserts frequently require hotter temperatures.

One thing that I have noticed is that clear skies at or near sea level is a very different thing from clear skies in the higher altitudes of New Mexico, Colorado, and Arizona. That extra 5000 feet of atmosphere at lower altitudes can diminish the oven's temperature somewhat, though the people in Wisconsin will tell you that they can still make some great solar foods!

* * *

For more information on solar cooking look for Rose's book "The Solar Chef" – available on Amazon.

Managing a Suburban Harvest

I live just south of the city of Albuquerque, New Mexico, on half an acre. This is a convenient halfway point for anyone who longs for a touch of country self-sufficiency but who may have a need to be near a larger population base for some reason.

The property is large enough for me to have a 50×60 vegetable garden, fruit trees, a beehive, and chickens. I enjoy organic gardening, canning, and otherwise processing the foods I eat all year. The problem is that although the harvest extends for a long time, I don't always have the time to pull down my canner.

Commercial farmers plant large areas and harvest everything at once – at the time they feel their plants have most of the produce at a perfect state of ripeness. Then everything gets trotted off for processing.

In my garden, I have 7 varieties of peppers, 2 types of tomatoes, green beans, lima beans, corn, cabbage, potatoes, onions, potatoes, peas, asparagus, broccoli, apples, pears, pecans, cherries, and a lot of herbs. They do not all ripen at once. (Thank heaven.)

Roasting Green Chile's on the Grill with oversight by Joe and Honey

Sometimes I can anticipate when a lot of one thing will be ready, but more often than not, things will ripen in stages. It is ridiculous to fire up the pressure canner for just a couple of quart jars. Not to mention that sometimes other personal responsibilities or vacation will supersede the joy of cooking and processing.

There are a few ways you can handle this with your kitchen garden to make it easier and more efficient.

Tomatoes are one of my favorite items to preserve – they are so versatile! Salsas, soups, sauces – YUM! The first luscious red fruits are sparse, but over time they pick up the pace. I plant just a few of the large beefsteak-type tomatoes, a couple cherry tomatoes, and 7 or 8 thicker paste tomatoes. Though the beefsteak and cherries are primarily for eating fresh, an overabundance of either can be added to the paste tomatoes when canning.

During those times when there are more ripe tomatoes than I have time to process, I will harvest and wash them, frequently cutting them into chunks and removing stems or spots. Then they get put into a gallon-sized Ziploc bag and plopped into the freezer.

Freezing at the peak of ripeness is a perfect way to build up enough of them for a good day of cooking and canning later on. I leave the nutritious skins on because tossing them in a food processor pulverizes them beautifully.

Another vegetable that you can partially process then freeze for future use is green chile peppers. Chiles are normally roasted and skinned before being cooked or canned. If you have a couple hours, you can pick the ones you feel are large enough and roast them on your BBQ grill. You want them to puff up and the skins to brown and crack a bit – but don't blacken them entirely!

You can grill at least a bucket full at a time. First soak the peppers for 1- 3 hours in water, then fire up the grill to high and toss them on. An option to turning them individually by hand is a grilling basket or rotisserie cage which allows you to turn them easier.

Take the roasted peppers and place them in a zip bag or other airtight container while they are still very hot and let them set in a warm place for a few hours or overnight. This is called "sweating" them, which helps separate the meat from the skins. Then plop them in the freezer.

Some people just leave them in the freezer until they wish to use them in cooking. I don't have enough freezer space to keep everything

I harvest there so I process as much as possible by canning. When you are ready to use them or can them, take them from the freezer to a clean kitchen sink. Fill the sink with water and when they thaw out you can begin stripping the skins from the peppers by hand.

Wearing rubber or latex gloves is a VERY good idea as the capsaicin in the peppers will make your hands burn after a while. I usually heavily cream my hands an hour before donning the gloves as an extra precaution.

Once the skins, stems and most of the seeds are removed you can either process them whole, chopped, or make great tasting sauces with them. I get heartburn from bell peppers and poblanos, but I have no problems with pimentos, cayenne, or green chile. As a result, my homemade spaghetti sauce has a mild bite to it, which south westerners appreciate.

Like most home farmers I love to pick my ears of corn just as they are fully ripe. If some of them escape my notice they can start to dry out a bit…or sometimes a lot. That's ok. When I find those I just let them continue to dry out until I am ready to use them. Then I shuck them and cut the kernels off and add them to homemade soups and stews.

If pollination has been spotty the corn cob may be partially bald. Rather than serve them on the cob I will cut the kernels off and freeze them. You can also freeze full cobs, but it takes a lot of freezer space.

Potatoes can be left in the ground long after the tops die back. A mild freeze late in fall won't usually hurt the ones that have a few inches of dirt over the top. Onions, carrots and garlic can just stay where they are all winter until I want to use them.

Broccoli is planted very early in the year – before the last frost date. It can handle a bit of cold. It creates one big head per plant, which commercial farmers harvest and send to the store before plowing the rest of the plant under. Personally, I think that is very premature. After I've harvested (and eaten) the main head I leave the plant in the ground where it will start to send out side shoots. You won't ever get another great big head, but the little shoots are great in salads and stir fry.

Cabbages are another plant that develop one huge head. However, the leaves around the main head are also edible and can be snipped off at any time for cole slaw, sauerkraut, or cabbage rolls.

In many climates, carrots, parsnips, turnips, garlic and onion seed or sets can be planted in the fall just before the first frost. Cover the beds in straw when nighttime freezes begin. You'd be amazed how many of them will be pushing up early next spring and ripe by June.

Of course, if you just have too much food on your hands at any given time, neighbors and local foodbanks will thank you for it. Giving away your extras makes a lot of friends!

***

Vegetable and Herbs that dry easily:

Celery
Onions
Carrots
Kale
Broccoli
Cauliflower
Garlic
Tomatoes
Corn
Peppers
Squash (Zukes and insides of winter squash and pumpkins

Herbs	**Other**
Sage	Fruit leathers
Basil	Peanuts
Oregano	Popcorn (certain varieties)
Mint	Pumpkin seeds
Rosemary	Sunflower Seeds
Thyme	Jerky
Savory	Vegetable leathers
Tarragon	

**For more information on food drying go to:
https://nchfp.uga.edu/how/dry**

Food Dehydration

What do you do if the vegetables you bought last week at the market start to look a little…dry? Do you just toss them out? There are other alternatives – the lease of which is simply adding them to your compost pile. True, some people – like inner city apartment dwellers – don't really have a composting option, but there are still uses for many types of dried vegetables. Why waste all that flavor?

If you live in an apartment the easiest way to dry foods is by using a countertop food dryer, or use your oven. The oven can get too hot for drying because most of them have a lowest setting of 170 degrees. You can crack it open a tad, which also helps heat the house in winter, but a ridiculous waste of energy in the summer.

If you have a solar oven that you cook with on your balcony or patio, it can also be used for drying foods. There are professionally designed solar ovens, or you can make and use ones yourself. The primary needs are a space that warms to about 120-130 degrees with a little airflow but does not allow access to insects or dirt. (If you park the car outside in the sun, setting a tray inside on a hot day does the trick pretty well, though drying onions, garlic, or herbs will leave behind a distinct aroma). Keep an outdoor thermometer near the food.

Of course, there are more options for people who own their own little piece of land.

Here in the Southwestern desert regions, we are blessed (cursed?) with abundant solar gain. One of the many ways we can use this resource is through dehydration of vegetables, fruits and meats.

For centuries humans have dried their foods in order to preserve and use them during the winter months. The knowledge of our ancestors combined with today's research has given us safe and yet creative methods of continuing this long tradition.

Left: A serious solar food dehydrator.

Inside racks of dehydrator.

Modify Your Garden Market Booth Tent

Do you enjoy taking your garden produce to market? Maybe you just want a shady spot while camping or at an event, and are more worried about high wind than rain – a common problem in the southwest. I've seen regular shade structures like the one in the photo picked up and thrown hundreds of feet away when a strong afternoon gust or mini-dust devil rolls through an event. I've seen these shelters picked up by afternoon desert winds and tossed around like a dog with a stuffed toy.

There is no reason at all why you can't take a regular big box store shade structure and modify it so it doesn't catch the wind like an umbrella. The 10×10-foot awnings available anywhere will provide shade. These are generically designed to protect from a light rain as well. Most of them have stakes to drive into the ground for stability from a light breeze but need to be anchored for protection from stronger gusts.

You can mitigate the wind flow problem by using several strategies for anchoring or modifying the standard structure. Ropes or bungees hooked to the upper corners and secured to cement bricks, or 5-gallon buckets or plastic tanks of water is a good start, if you are allowed to set up next to a truck you can anchor to it as well. Even then you'll get some significant pulling when the wind scoops up from underneath. Even if the structure stays in place the wind can warp or damage the poles.

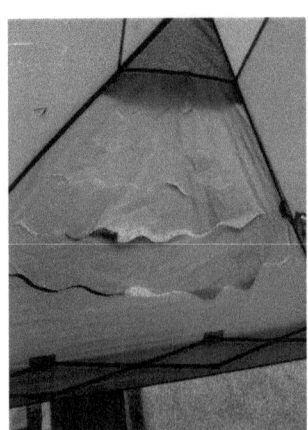

There is another modification that significantly lessens the winds ability to pull the structure. Set it up and using a very sharp knife, make some V shaped or wave shaped slits in the fabric roof. My daughter and I carved several different patterns into one of our structures and they work very well. Also, in order to "hide" the modifications, we used acrylic paint to create a nice mountain picture on the outside of the roof.

The next time I set up to do some solar cooking demonstrations my structure withstood the afternoon winds significantly better than the others in the area. While neighbors grabbed for the anchor posts frequently, the wind fluttered through and escaped through the venting. We don't often have to worry about heavy rain here, and the structure will still tolerate a mild rain without soaking people and items inside.

****

A Practical Environmentalist

"What are you doing?" I asked my daughter. After living with me for 13 years, you'd think that she would automatically toss her aluminum soda can into the recycle bin. No, it was airborne and headed into the trash when the flash of sunlight on metal caught my eye.

Rolling her eyes, she fished the can out and put it in the right place.

The Right Place. Sometimes I catch myself thinking about how much has changed – not just technology or building developments, but mindsets. Growing up in the 1960's I would not have thought about where I threw any can. At that time, there were no soda cans, just bottles. Even then my parents did not purchase sodas for their kids except as occasional treats; we drank water, milk or Kool-Aid. Hawaiian Punch was a treat served only on holidays.

In my parents' youth everything was used, re-used and then torn apart and used some other way before it was ever thrown away. That was before advancements in technology turned us into a "throw away" society. Plastic was one of the biggest culprits. Suddenly you could make anything so cheaply that you didn't have to bother to clean it up and use it again – just throw it away! Who cares – it's only worth about a nickel and what's a nickel?

I grew up in the suburbs, Indianapolis, Minneapolis, Chicago, and Louisville – they were all pretty much the same in the 1960s and 70s. The paved streets were shaded by overhanging branches, and illumined by yellowish streetlights that attracted clouds of moths and bugs each evening. Ranch style homes boasted big yards with no fences, every week Dad and the neighbor took turns mowing a long strip along the mostly undefined boundaries.

There were flower gardens, but only an occasional small vegetable plot. Dad always had a couple tomato plants tucked out of sight along the side of the house. A big metal barrel along the back of the property was where we burned our paper trash, and garbage was picked up from the stinky, smelly trash can set outside once a week. Luckily, I had four sisters, so there were a lot of hands sharing the dishwashing duties. My brother, being a guy, was excused from kitchen work. (But he did have to take out the trash!).

Every morning Mom slathered peanut butter and jelly on Wonder Bread, folded each sandwich in a napkin, put them in paper bags and handed them to us as we ran out the door to the school bus stop. Breakfast was a bowl of cereal, drinks were kool-aid or ice tea. Mom, sometimes Dad, would cook dinner every night. It was usually something high in carbs like tuna and noodles, meatloaf and potatoes, or spaghetti. Once a week, if we were lucky, we got to go to Burger Chef for dinner – FRENCH FRIES and COLAS!

Like most of middle America, my parents saw advances in technology that made life easier as wonderful. For years during the summer, my siblings and I would come out of our bedrooms and sleep on the floor of the living room or hall – wherever we could find a cool spot. Air conditioning was installed about the time I got into high school – Wow!

One of the most welcome innovations was the plastic bag. Finally, a "clean" way of disposing of trash! Sandwich bags had foldover tops at first. When the Ziploc-type closures were added, Mom would buy a box and wash them by hand until they could not be used anymore. I think that is the first "sustainable" action by today's definition, that I remember. Taking something that was designed to be disposable and re-using it.

Somewhere in the 1970s, it suddenly dawned on people here in the good ol' USA that just maybe all that waste was bad for us. By "us" I mean not just the country as a whole but towns and communities that don't have any place to bury their trash. Some places have to pay to have their garbage shipped to other places with smaller populations and more land.

During that era we discovered that splitting the atom may have created huge new energy resources, but the process creates more garbage of a kind that can make people sick. Then there are the fools who want to live in the southwestern desert, but believe in their souls that they have the right to use as much water as they want so they can have a lush green yard.

Technology has spoiled us on a number of levels. You go to a grocery store these days and you can get any kind of fruit or vegetable at any time of year. You want fresh tomatoes in January, corn on the cob in April, young tender zucchini anytime…why not? So what if it takes a jumbo jet out of Hawaii plus a huge tractor trailer driving 1,072 miles to bring you fresh pineapple in Amarillo, where it costs only a couple bucks at the store. From picking to purchase it costs the world 9504 gallons of Jet fuel, and at least 180 gallons of diesel. That's a lot of dirty chemicals dumped into the air we breathe.

Like a lot of people, I have absorbed all the statistics and come to the realization that we as individuals really do need to change how we approach everything from what food-gathering options we have to how we dispose of waste. What bugs me is that the minute you mention that you save aluminum cans or recycle computer paper, people automatically equate you with the wild-eyed frenetic extremists who sit in trees and scream obscenities at passing loggers.

Applause to the radicals who bring attention to a problem. It is not how I prefer to live. They may draw attention to a situation, but it is the average citizen living in a community who will slowly and steadily change it. People need to look around and see what they personally can do in daily life to make a difference.

I am an inhabitant of the high desert. My home includes just under an acre of land in a rural part of Bernalillo County, New Mexico. The community is large enough to have a choice of waste disposal companies and I prefer to use one that recycles.

As I mentioned before, when my company transferred me to Albuquerque, I met a wonderful group of people who taught me the concept of "green living". I became a member of the New Mexico Solar Energy Association and through my association with these environmental gurus, I learned to examine all aspects of my life as it relates to the welfare of the planet.

Having two young daughters of my own at that time, I did not cast off the trappings of middle-class suburban existence overnight to embrace the practices of self-styled privation sometimes referred to as the "good life". But I began to consciously study ways to incorporate sustainable actions in our daily routines. We began with collecting our aluminum cans rather than just throwing them away.

I read Organic Gardening and Mother Earth News. Houses in Albuquerque have yards that are much smaller than back in the Midwest, and every one of them is surrounded by rock or cement walls. I rented a rototiller and ripped out a part of the backyard to create an organic garden. Now I would be able to feed healthier meals to my kids. I built a compost bin and became a successful "leaf thief". I don't drink coffee, but Starbucks became a frequent stop on my way home from work – by that time they usually had a ton of used grounds to give away.

The house was also chosen because it was only a couple blocks away from the kids' school and a couple blocks the other direction to a grocery store. Walking or bicycling assumed an importance that they had not had since I first earned a driver's license.

Luckily, I did not live in an area subject to the restrictions of a homeowner's association, and with the walls around the back yard the neighbor's never objected to my use of a "solar" clothes dryer. Although I had a fire pit with a grill in the yard, I fell in love with solar ovens – the concept that you could cook a meal with sunlight!!! Wow!

Piece by piece, bit by bit, I have made changes in my lifestyle to reflect a conscious decision to reduce the impact of my existence on the planet. I turn down the heat in winter and wear more sweaters, not because I can't afford the utility bill but because it means less pollution. I donate time, and money, to those environmental organizations that I feel are making a difference in our world. Do I intend to sell my house and leave behind all the advantages of civilization…no. But I do purchase "green" energy credits, drive a hybrid car with over 300,000 miles, and bug my congress people to vote responsibly.

The New Mexico Solar Energy Association has been keeping the flame of sustainable living alive ever since the Reagan administration had ripped away the solar tax credits introduced by Carter. Every year they used to have a conference at a retreat up in northern New Mexico where the membership would talk passive solar, active solar, wind energy, solar cooking, etc.. It was a fun reunion of like-minded individuals, but it was singing to the choir.

About ten years ago I worked with the group to create a venue for middle-class homeowners which would allow them to taste and investigate the wonders of renewable energy and sustainable living. The Solar Fiesta was born, and the citizens of central New Mexico embraced it. The event incorporates a greater variety of green concepts and ideals in a hands on fun fashion. Exhibits, demonstrations and workshops are designed to intrigue the average homeowner and lead children and adults toward a future green ideal are the norm rather than merely interesting.

Practical Environmentalism begins with understanding at a deep level that there is a need for change, then instituting those changes incrementally, but steadily, so that over time they become a part of who you are. Thirty years later, my daughter and I were at a card party. As we sat there a member of the opposing team chucked his aluminum soda can into the trash. We both flinched, looked at each other and grinned.

***

The wood from this box was originally used to ship auto glass. The sides are made of 2x8in planks. The bottom of the bed is lined with 2 inches of cardboard donated by a friend who recently got new kitchen appliances and some shipping boxes.
Over time it is being layers with coffee grounds, grass clippings, kitchen compost, straw and garden refuse like the outer leaves of cabbages seen here.

Scavenger Gardening

If you like pretty neat gardens with identical beds and shiny pots that could have come out from Tiffany's, throw this book away right now.

Scavenger Gardening means seeing and using materials that are already around you. It is the ultimate in recycle, reuse, etc... It does not mean your garden has to be ugly, but if done correctly it will be unique.

Living sustainably and recycling wasn't even a "thing" when I was a kid growing up in the suburban Midwest. Yet somewhere deep in my soul was a homesteader – a person who doesn't feel that just throwing things a way and buying new stuff all the time is right. That's like throwing away your money!

I remember seeing a play at the local community theater when I was about 8 years old. It was called *Everybody Loves Opal* – a comedy about an older lady who lived alone on the outskirts of town. She was a sweetheart who scrimped and saved any way she could. A trio of would-be crooks conned their way into hiding out at her place after a heist. They kept being confused because she had old jars and tin cans all over the place with things inside. Yard sale canisters and wooden boxes not only contained the usual coffee, tea, and sugar. Some were full of buttons, or seeds, or coins, or whatever she found as she walked over by the city dump that was useful.

I thought that was so cool!

Next Valentines Day I asked Mom if I could keep the big heart shaped chocolates box she got from Dad when it was empty. That became a repository for small pretty stones I found wandering the neighborhood and later a place to put newspaper photos of my teenage heartthrobs – Ilya Kuryakin and Mr. Spock.

It's not like the concept of recycling or reusing things is new. My father's oldest brother's youngest daughter was a few years older than I was – which meant I got some really cool clothes as hand-me-downs! I wish you could still take glass bottles of soda someplace where they pay you a penny apiece and have them truly reused rather than melted down after just one person drinks from them.

The advantages of recycling have finally gotten through to most of the population, but before it is tossed in the recycle bin you might consider how daily items could be reused first.

I love containers – all kinds. As an urban homesteader, I find all kinds of uses for the types of things most people either throw out or toss in a recycle bin. Last week I noticed a couple plastic boxes sitting next to a dumpster. They were about two feet long, six inches wide and six inches deep. Perfect for transporting small potted plants. One is currently in my refrigerator holding garden produce and another is sitting in my sunroom planted with leaf lettuce.

My co-workers take turns bringing in large plastic containers of pretzels or crunchy cheese balls for office munching. When empty no one really wants them, but no one wants to throw them away, so when I joined the group, six containers sat on top of the refrigerator. Five of them came home with me that night, one was put to an alternate use in the office.

That pretzel jar is now stationed next to the coffee maker with the word "Grounds" marked on the side. The staff quickly took to tossing all the coffee grounds with the filters into the jar. When it is full, (about twice a week) I trade it out and take the full one home. The grounds go into the compost heap, the jar is cleaned up and waits to be taken back to the office.

My husband has a passion for screwdrivers. He never seems to have enough, and he never seems to be able to find exactly the right one – even though he has three big toolboxes. One of the pretzel jars has become a repository for screwdrivers. I find them around the house and toss them in the jar. Since it is clear plastic, it's easy for him to see the tools.

The base of the jars is about 9 inches in diameter; if you cut the jar in half, the base can be used under a flowerpot in the sunroom. The upper half can be placed around a garden plant, like a tomato. Push the cut edge down into the dirt to discourage slugs, roly polys and hornworms. Turn a whole jar upside down over a young plant to create a mini-greenhouse. Be sure to put a stone on top to keep it from falling over.

They make great containers for bags of rice, macaroni, dried beans, cookies, sugar, or anything traditionally kept in a canister. The size of the mouth makes it easy to scoop out just the amount you need.

One item I enjoy picking up at yard sales are the old metal food canisters. These were created to store foods such as popcorn and cookies. They come in all sizes, and you can use them for storing a plethora of items that don't sit well in plastic. Some things I've stored include bars of homemade soap, beef jerky, oatmeal and rice.

Many people have regular medications they take which come from the pharmacy in amber colored plastic tube containers. These come in a variety of sizes and are excellent for storing seeds. Be sure to air dry the seeds well prior to storage and use a permanent market to record the type of seed and date stored. You can paint over the pharmacy names on the caps. If moisture is a concern, add small moisture packs before closing.

Slats from old plastic window blinds can be cut into 6-inch-long pieces and used as row markers in a garden. Just write on them with permanent markers. White plastic forks and knives from restaurant takeout are good for that too.

Keep the twine from any straw bales you buy for mulching. It's perfect for dozens of garden projects, from tying up tomatoes to dangling from above for beans, peas, and cucumbers to climb.

Keep all those cups you get from fast food joints. Paper and plastic can both be cleaned out, filled with potting soil, and used to start seeds.

Large bags of potting soil, mulch, or garden soil are easily recycled – most easily fit in a tall kitchen trash can.

These are but a few of the many ways you can save money and contribute to reducing waste through scavenger gardening. For more ideas on ways to live sustainably, over the next few pages, I've gone into more detail on these and other ways to save money by repurposing products that would otherwise be consigned to the trash bin.

For example: plastic straws. Many communities are banning local restaurants from automatically providing their customers with plastic straws because so many end up in landfills or floating in the ocean along with flimsy cheap plastic cups and lids. You don't have to just use them once. I put mine in the tableware part of a dishwasher and

use them over and over along with the cups and lids. They only go into the recycle bin when they become unusable.

A restaurant near me serves their beverages in sturdy plastic cups with strong lids and straws that frequently survive an unexpected drop on the ground. These are the kind of cups you really want to keep around. They used to refill these large cups for less than a dollar until Covid restrictions stopped that practice. I have dozens squirreled away which I use at home whenever I plan to work out in the hot sun for a few hours. They make great travel cups.

Other drink cups are just the right size to plant seeds in during February that will be set out in the garden come April. All they need is a drainage hole. I set them in the sunroom in big plastic boxes and usually have more than enough to share with friends and fellow gardeners.

Gardeners like to rejuvenate their soil in the spring by adding some composted manure or topsoil and some buy potting soil in large bags. Others buy big bags of mulching materials. (Some people buy dog food or other animal foods packaged in 30 to 50 lb bags)

Don't just throw them away! Once they are emptied out, neatly cut off the top part of the bag and use them for trash. I keep a stack of neatly folded ones for weed collecting – especially when the weeds have big seed heads that I do NOT want in my compost bin. You don't have to wash them out to use them as trash can liners in the garage and you save money on commercial plastic garbage bags.

People with medical issues are saddled with unrecyclable plastic prescription bottles in varying sizes. The uses for them are legion! Gardeners who collect seeds from year-to-year love that the amber colored plastic helps protect viability.

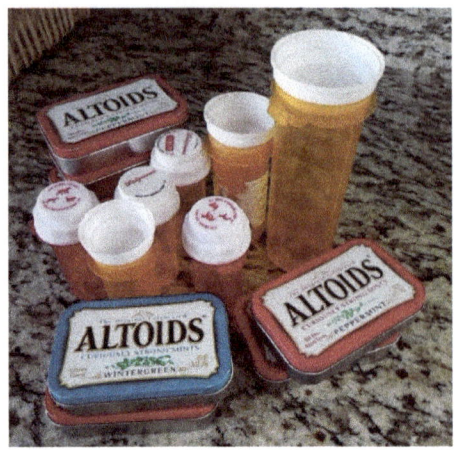

Altoid tins are infinitely useful. they are great for storing pins/needles, fishing flies, paper clips, jewelry, and bobby pins. You can protect wooden matches while traveling, and keep anything away that might want to nibble on your soap while camping. Fill them with pins, buttons, paperclips, earrings, rings, spices, and any number of other items that might need a little more protection than a regular box. You can spray paint them and use a marker to label the contents.

They are also fun kid-project boxes.

Plastic drink cups are just the right size to plant seeds in during February that will be set out in the garden come April. All they need is a drainage hole. I set them in the sunroom in big plastic boxes and usually have more than enough to share with friends and fellow gardeners.

Every time you go to a fast food place and buy a drink you have what you need to start new plants. Instead of throwing away the drink cups, take them home and drill holes in the bottom and fill with seed starting mix. Use them for cutting transplants or to start seedlings. The deep cup lets roots grow downwards. If you use clear cold drink cups you can watch the roots as they expand and grow.

I love to take old pillowcases and keep them in the car – especially during the summer. If you have to park with the windshield facing the steering wheel just toss the pillowcase over the wheel to keep from frying your hands when you get back in the car.

Did you just finish a small drywall project? Those 1-gallon spackle or drywall compound buckets are great to use when you don't need a really big bucket.

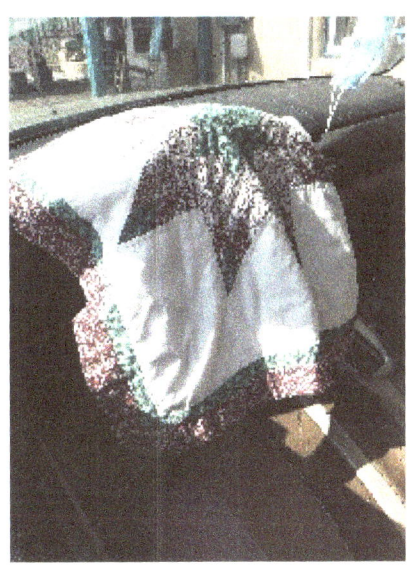

You know those large clear plastic tops that come on cakes and croissants at the grocery store? They make great mini greenhouse caps for seeds you put out now. They are helping my cold tolerant seeds like spinach, snow peas, and lettuce to break ground, and keep them just warm enough at night so that the occasional cold plunge is not harming them. To stabilize them from the wind set a rock on top.

I also use the plastic tops and trays from takeout meals from restaurants. They are usually large enough to act as water catch basins below indoor planter pots.

Some good restaurants for sturdy two piece To-Go boxes:

Olive Garden's Soup box
Chedder's
Burritos Alistante
Genghis Grill
Pizza 9
The Range Cafe
Long John Silvers

Several restaurants which serve soups, have *To Go* plastic containers with lids in pint and quart sizes.

Smaller plastic containers which can be used for dipping sauces, chopped onions and peppers can be found at Kentucky Fried Chicken.

Do you need row labels to figure out where the carrots end and the beets begin? Save the wooden sticks from popsicles or use old plastic window blinds. Cut the blinds using a regular pair of scissors into 8-inch strips. Cut off the cord and wind it up for use elsewhere – like to tie up vines on a trellis. Write the name of the plant on the strips with a permanent marker or ball point pen and stick it into the ground. (A ball point pen will leave behind an imprint in the plastic even if the ink washes off.

A trip to Goodwill can help you with setting up microclimates in your garden. Pick up lengths of thin window curtain sheers to use as shade over your garden. Old child/pet gates can be set up sideways as trellises for beans and peas.

Last year's hard plastic small child swimming pool makes a good bed for shallow rooted plants like lettuce, kale, onions, spinach etc. After a season of cooling kids off on a summer day these pools can develop small cracks in the bottom making them unusable for more pool frolicking, but just right for shallow gardens. I end up adding a few more cracks or drill holes for drainage to keep the plants from root rot.

Old, used 55-gallon (food grade) plastic barrels have a number of possible uses. They can be modified into rain barrels or turn them sideways to create top bar-style bee hives. Cutting them in half creates two tubs – essentially large planters. The top part comes with holes for drainage, but you will have to drill them in the bottom part. I like to paint the outsides with fun colors.

If you have a family member who receives medications which need to stay cool via the mail, they are often sent in large thick plastic or Styrofoam containers.

Old waterbed frames are very sturdy and only need to be set up outside on the ground and filled with dirt. Other furniture can be recycled into planters. Some suggestions are bookshelves, dressers and dresser drawers. Avoid using furniture constructed using thinner walled wood, particle board or plastic as it will fall apart easily.

Unusual items such as old sinks, wagons and pickup trucks can add visual interest to your raised bed areas. I've seen planters made from old BBQ grills and toilets that were painted in whimsical fashion.

Old acrylic signs, such as realtor's use, can be set on the west side of a plant to give it shade in the heat of an afternoon. Brassicas love that.

If you know a beekeeper, he usually has a lot of old wooden boxes no longer usable for the bees, but they are still sturdy enough to plant in.

Where can you find materials needed for these innovative growing structures? It can be simply a matter of keeping your eyes and ears open. A friend had a deck built on the front of his permanently parked recreational vehicle. When he no longer had a use for it, he gave the structure to me. I took the boards from the top and reset them on the sides of the structure making it into a raised bed.

Businesses that make custom windows often receive large sheets of glass in sturdy wood boxes. Frequently made of 2x10's that are 6 to 8 feet in length, the businesses have no use for the shipping boxes once the glass is removed. These may need some extra wood or other material to fill gaps between boards, but the basic structure is very sound. I used leftover strips of vinyl floor laminate from a kitchen project on the inside wall to cover and waterproof the gaps.

Wind baffles can be constructed from leftover cinderblocks, old trellising, or fabric lined wire fencing. You can also set branches, sticks or bamboo poles in the ground on the windward side of your garden bed.

If you have a friend who is doing some home remodeling, he might be very happy to have you cart away the old bathtub or carpet. Cutting the carpet into long strips that fit perfectly between the garden beds cuts back on weeds.

Cheap lengths of sheer fabric, like window curtains, from yard sales and goodwill are an economical way to create canopies for garden beds. They may only last a season – especially with the high winds we get but are easily replaced.

Old storm doors with windows and screens are fairly lightweight. You can set them over a long bed to create an instant cold frame.

Large truck tires can be stacked and filled with soil for a novel raised bed that heats up quickly in the spring. I have also seen old commodes turned into interesting yard art!

Many times, people still keep the metal **structure of a shade tent**, even though the canopy material has ripped over time. That metal structure can be covered by heavy plastic to make a greenhouse! The one in the photo below served me well for the 3 years I lived at 7,560 feet in the Sandia Mountains.

***

In my handbag you can usually find a small plastic food storage box-the kind you can re-use. If I know the restaurant's leftover containers are Styrofoam, I pull my box out and use it instead. Many of the containers I carry came from other restaurants – taken home and washed to re-use as needed. Did you know that the small containers Kentucky Fried Chicken uses for single servings of cole slaw make great butter dishes?

The water in my community is tasty. I run it through a filter and drink it rather than buying a lot of plastic water bottles. That does not mean I shun any use of plastic ones. There are times when that is preferable to other options and I do keep, clean, and re-use any that do come my way.

My husband and I prefer to buy locally, but if price differences are dramatically different, we don't have any prejudices about bopping over to Wal-Mart. My own organic garden and the local Farmer's Market provide most of my vegetables, and I like to can and dehydrate my produce. The garden is on a drip system, and I employ heavy mulching, so my water usage is much smaller than my neighbor with the lawn.

The most amazingly short-sighted waste is in the area of clothing. People keep closets full of things they don't wear, or if they've worn it once or torn it slightly, they may throw it away! If something is torn, I pull out needle and thread and stitch it up, then wear it again! Twice a year I take inventory of what I have. If I haven't worn it because I got too fat or don't like it anymore, I give it to charity. You can get some really great clothes at thrift stores – from those people who wore it once.

I own a total of six pairs of boots/shoes. Sas shoes has a very practical black leather shoe I can wear all day long in the office and be comfortable. They are expensive but great. Once a year I buy a new pair. The old pair becomes my gardening shoes. I keep a pair of brown loafers, a pair of black pumps going on nine years old, some comfortable Skechers, and a pair of winter boots over 20 years old that are handy if I take a ski trip up to the top of .Sandia Mountain.

Creating a healthier environment starts in the mind. Look around and see what you can do in your own home to make a difference. Start small, but do it repeatedly until it becomes a habit.

Reuse Before Recycle.

The mantra of sustainable. living, reduce, reuse, recycle...is old hat to those whose families and lifestyles are well away from most towns and cities. It is only within the past century or so that corporations have been able to offer us the convenience of fresh vegetables in the marketplace all years long. The development of plastic may arguably be the one invention that changed our lifestyle more than anything else.

Like many who prefer to live lightly on the planet I cannot argue that plastic has earned its place, but I try to put it in perspective by not succumbing to the temptation to use it and throw it away if possible.

My preference is to use those plastics which are more likely to break down quickly rather than languor for decades in a landfill. There are companies like Cleanomics that make plastic bags designed to do exactly that. I also look for alternative ways of using rather than trashing many other items.

One of the best arguments for sustainable living is that it is also the best way to save money. In their mania to buy whatever item is currently popular or fashionable, (and therefore expensive) many people fritter away their hard-earned cash.

One day while visiting Indiana I watched a 10-year-old nephew flipping a cell phone and tossing it in the air. He'd drop it on the ground then go back to flipping it until he dropped it again. I asked him how many hours had his parents worked to pay for the cell phone? He looked at me like I was nuts.

That is the secret really, unless someone is born rich it is important for us to remember, and to teach our children, that the things we want don't just magically appear out of thin air.

So, in the spirit of personal frugality and social responsibility I offer a few hints and tips.

Bakery plastic boxes. If someone gets croissants or muffins from most grocery store bakeries, they come in clear plastic boxes. Use these under flowerpots or use as a soap mold. Can contain items you intend to giftwrap. Stackable.

Cardboard Boxes – uses of cardboard are endless. After removing whatever has been shipped to me I assess the boxes condition and size then determine if I should:

- Store the box for future shipping
- Flatten and store it for the next time I create garden beds
- Tear it up into smaller pieces to create soil sponges
- Leave it out for my pets to play with
- Shred it for small animal cage litter.
- Large ones can be spread under a car to catch oil leaks
- Coffins for small critters

Milk Crates are heavy duty plastic formed into squares or rectangles about 10 inches high. These crates are great for transporting anything that is heavy and does not need to be waterproof.

Similar crates were made for transporting bottled liquids like soft drinks. They are a convenient size for moving books, jars, bottles, and small boxes.

Office Shredder: Most paper and ink is non-toxic. If you have a large compost bin you can take the confetti made by an office shredder and toss it with other materials. This is especially good in summer when most of the material is green and needs balancing. It also makes good packing material for shipping.

Office Coffeepot: Place a large plastic container – like one of the ones pretzels come in from Costco or Sam's – next to the office coffeepot with the words "Coffee Grounds" written on the side. In short order everyone will be throwing the grounds into the convenient jar. Take them home and either bury around the plants or toss in compost heap for later. The filters are compostable too, but I usually soak the grounds off of them if I want to add the grounds directly to my roses.

Pretzel Containers: Speaking of those big clear containers, they are large enough for a lot of things:

- Great place to store all sizes of screwdrivers, electrical outlets and switches, power cords
- Cut the thing in two. Use the bottom half under flowerpots, set the top half over seedlings in the garden to protect them from bugs and high winds.
- Empty the large bags of dried beans, peanuts, or rice into them for ease of use.
- Cut a small hole in the lid. Put yarn inside and draw out through hole. Keeps kids, cats, and puppies out.

Freezer: The freezer uses less energy if it is full. If it has gaps, fill plastic jugs with water and set them inside until you order the next side of beef.

Plastic Zip Loc Bags: I prefer to get the heavy-duty freezer style bags. You can buy meat in larger quantities to save money, cut it into sections and freeze for later. These are sturdy enough to wash, rinse with a bit of bleach, dry and use again.

***

My mother was born in the mid 1930's, so she was old enough to remember how people supported the war efforts during WWII. Whenever canned goods were used, people removed the paper wrapping then cut out both the bottom and top lids. Then the round can would be squashed flat. All these along with the aluminum wrappers on bubble gum would be set aside so they could be melted and recase into airplane and ship parts for the war.

Many foodstuffs were rationed, so most of the people in towns and suburbs kept vegetable gardens along with rabbits or chickens to supplement their meals.

Children today frequently grow up in households where the mindset is "use and throw away". Many homes don't keep a sewing box to handle small tears in clothing, and they'd rather toss something than have to wash and use it again. We have become lazy and short-sighted, and I pray that our society does not suffer a meltdown which would throw them into a panic.

For you and me, the rewards of sustainable living and gardening are far reaching. We create communities that can support themselves and each other. I give vegetables from my yard to my neighbor who sends me her extra eggs, and I donate some to the local food bank.

***

Do you have some more good tips on gardening, reusing, or sustainable living techniques? Send them along and I may post them on my website.

Email to: solarranch@swcp.com

Other Books by Rose Marie Kern available on Amazon

The Solar Chef

A guide to cooking with sunlight, The Solar Chef was distributed worldwide and endorsed by Sun Ovens International. Now in it's 8th edition, the Solar Chef contains information on how to cook with sunlight along with recipes from breakfast to dessert!

This updated edition also includes gluten free recipes.

The Secret to Creating Microclimates for High Desert Gardening

Master Gardener Rose Kern combines her skills as a professional weather forecaster with observations and experiences gained from living in high desert areas for over 40 years. Her information and advice are delivered in a format friendly to new gardeners.

Rosie Kern

Rose Marie (Rosie) Kern has been a gardener since she was eight years old. As an adult, her job moved her from Indiana to Albuquerque and she discovered that not all growing conditions are the same. That stimulated her to obsess over garden books and organic living magazines. Her practical gardening education lead her to become a member of the USDA's Albuquerque Area Extension Master Gardeners.

In addition to her gardening expertise, Rose has a lifetime's worth of knowledge and experience with solar and sustainable living techniques and working with non-profits. She has two books and hundreds of articles for such magazines as Mother Earth News, Countryside, Solar Today and Backwoods Home. Her book on solar cooking is in its 8th edition.

She will tell you, "Organically grown food cooked in a solar oven is the best there is!"

www.solaranch.com

USDA National Institute of Food and Agriculture
U.S. DEPARTMENT OF AGRICULTURE

USDA Extension Master Gardener volunteers share their gardening knowledge by teaching workshops, managing demonstration and community gardens, speaking at events and staffing garden information helplines. According to the most recent reports, the more than 89,000 EMG volunteers contributed 4.9 million hours in community volunteerism in 2023, valued at $157 million in donated time nationwide. These volunteers collectively reached 10 million people through their work.

https://www.nifa.usda.gov/about-nifa/blogs/master-gardeners-help-provide-solutions-gardeners

ALBUQUERQUE AREA EXTENSION MASTER GARDENERS

We are community volunteers trained in horticulture by the New Mexico State University Cooperative Extension Service.

We can help you understand the science of the various soils in our area and tell you what grows best here. We can help with those pesky entomology, or bug, problems. We have up-to-date information about plant botany, plant diseases, growing fruits and vegetables, caring for your lawn, and growing roses. Are you interested in xeriscaping? We have information about that as well. We are here to help you develop gardens that will thrive and be beautiful in our arid landscape.
www.abqmastergardeners.org

Become a Master Gardener!

For almost 50 years, Extension Master Gardeners (EMG) have educated millions about sustainable and environmentally friendly garden practices. The United States Department of Agriculture's (USDA) National Institute of Food and Agriculture (NIFA) provides crucial support to the Extension Master Gardener program through capacity funding to Extension programs in all 50 states and the District of Columbia.

The Master Gardener's program exists throughout the United States. Everyday citizens can take expert level classes to help improve their own gardening in exchange for volunteering their time and expertise to their communities. It was created and organized by the U.S. Department of Agriculture.

How Master Gardeners Get the Job Done

- Teaching workshops
- Staffing garden information hotlines
- Managing demonstration and community gardens
- Speaking at events
- Partnering with organizations like 4-H to bring garden and food production skills to wider audiences.

Master Gardeners reached more than 8.4 million people directly in 2020, according to the 2020 Extension Master Gardener Impact Report. Their work totaled more than 3 million volunteer hours—with a value of more than $76 million.

For more information on the USDA Master Gardener program go to:
https://www.nifa.usda.gov/about-nifa/blogs/master-gardeners-numbers

www.ingramcontent.com/pod-product-compliance
Lightning Source LLC
Chambersburg PA
CBHW061219070526
44584CB00029B/3892